AROUND new york city WITH KIDS

2nd Edition

by Mindy Bailin

Fodor's Travel Publications
New York • Toronto • London • Sydney • Auckland

www.fodors.com

Credits
Writer: Mindy Bailin

Series Editors: Karen Cure, Andrea Lehman
Editor: Andrea Lehman
Editorial Production: Marina Padakis
Production/Manufacturing: Colleen Ziemba

Design: Fabrizio La Rocca, *creative director;*
Tigist Getachew, *art director*
Illustration and Series Design: Rico Lins, Keren Ora
Adomoni/Rico Lins Studio

About the Writer
New Yorker Mindy Bailin is a teacher and mother of three
who writes frequently about family, education, and health
for many newspapers and magazines across the country.

Fodor's Around New York City with Kids

Second Edition
ISBN 0–679–00915–9
ISSN 1526–1468

Important Tip
Although all prices, opening times, and other details in this
book are based on information supplied to us at press time,
changes occur all the time in the travel world, and Fodor's
cannot accept responsibility for facts that become outdat-
ed or for inadvertent errors or omissions. So always confirm
information when it matters, especially if you're making a
detour to visit a specific place.

Special Sales
Fodor's Travel Publications are available at special discounts for bulk purchases for sales promotions or premi-
ums. Special editions, including personalized covers,
excerpts of existing guides, and corporate imprints, can be
created in large quantities for special needs. For more information, contact your local bookseller or Special Markets,
Fodor's Travel Publications, 280 Park Avenue, New York, NY
10017. Inquiries from Canada should be directed to your
local Canadian bookseller or sent to Random House of
Canada, Ltd., Marketing Dept., 2775 Matheson Boulevard
East, Mississauga, Ontario L4W 4P7. Inquiries from the
United Kingdom should be sent to Fodor's Travel
Publications, 20 Vauxhall Bridge Road, London, England
SW1V 2SA.

PRINTED IN THE UNITED STATES OF AMERICA
10 9 8 7 6 5 4 3 2 1

COUNTDOWN TO GOOD TIMES

Get Ready, Get Set!

68 American Folk Art Museum

67 American Museum of Natural History

66 American Museum of the Moving Image

65 Asphalt Green

64 Broadway on a Budget

63 Bronx Zoo

62 Brooklyn Academy of Music

61 Brooklyn Botanic Garden

60 Brooklyn Children's Museum

59 Brooklyn Museum of Art

58 Carnegie Hall

57 Castle Clinton National Monument

56 Central Park

55 Central Park Zoo

54 Chelsea Piers

53 Children's Museum of Manhattan

52 Children's Museum of the Arts

51 Clay Pit Ponds State Park Preserve

50 Colden Center for the Performing Arts
49 Coney Island
48 Ellis Island
47 Empire State Building
46 F.A.O. Schwarz
45 Federal Hall National Memorial
44 Forbes Magazines Galleries
43 Fraunces Tavern Museum
42 Historic Richmond Town
41 Intrepid Sea Air Space Museum
40 Jewish Museum
39 Jones Beach State Park
38 Liberty Science Center
37 Lower East Side Tenement Museum
36 Madame Tussaud's Wax Museum
35 Madison Square Garden
34 Metropolitan Museum of Art
33 Museum of Modern Art
32 Museum of Television and Radio

31 Museum of the City of New York

30 National Museum of the American Indian

29 NBC Studios Backstage Tour

28 New Victory Theater

27 New York Aquarium

26 New York Botanical Garden

25 New York City Fire Museum

24 New York City Opera Young People's Workshops

23 New York Hall of Science

22 New-York Historical Society

21 New York Liberty Basketball

20 New York Transit Museum

19 New York Unearthed

18 NY Waterway Ferries

17 PlaySpace

16 Prospect Park

15 Prospect Park Zoo

14 Puppetworks

13 Queens County Farm Museum

12 Queens Zoo

11 Radio City Music Hall

10 Rockefeller Center and the Ice Rink

9 Rye Playland

8 Schomburg Center

7 Sony Wonder Technology Lab

6 South Street Seaport Museum

5 Staten Island Children's Museum

4 Staten Island Zoo

3 Statue of Liberty

2 Theodore Roosevelt Birthplace

1 United Nations

Extra! Extra!

High Fives

Play While You Wait

Good Times Galore

Something for Everyone

All Around Town

Many Thanks!

GET READY, GET SET!

Go ahead. Take a bite of the Big Apple and count down to fun while you visit the 68 places that appear in this handy-dandy collection of favorite places and spaces to explore. Whether you're day tripping in the city, planning a weekend family getaway, or spending a weeklong vacation here, there's no better place to be than N-Y-C (or the entire metropolitan area surrounding the city, if you really want to know). These 68 great things to do together include sites in Manhattan, as well as Brooklyn, the Bronx, Queens, and Staten Island. A few sights in New Jersey and Westchester and on Long Island are also included. They're only a stone's throw from the Big Apple and worth the trip.

LOOK INSIDE

Each two-page spread in this book describes a great place to take your family. The "tool bar" at the top of the page lists all the particulars: address, phone numbers, admission prices, hours, and age recommendations. "Keep in Mind" boxes give parents special information to help them make the most of their excursion, while "Hey, Kids!" points out cool facts just for kids. "Eats for Kids" helps you find family-friendly restaurants nearby.

Also in the tool bar are Web addresses for most attractions. Some sites offer virtual tours of these great destinations, which may get your family in the mood for a "field trip." Many Web sites also include learning activities, background information on exhibits, and calendars of events, classes, and programs open to the public. It's worth a look before you plan your visit, and after you go, these sites can be great resources for kids who want to learn more.

To get started, just flip through the book, keeping an eye peeled for the Statue of Liberty's magical transformation. It could only happen in New York. You can find places that are right for your family by just leafing through the listings (in alphabetical order) or by looking in the directories in the back of the book. "All Around Town" groups sights by neighborhood, helpful if you are planning to visit more than one attraction or are looking for additional kid-friendly dining choices. (Call ahead for travel directions and parking availability.) "Something for Everyone" groups attractions by type, such as parks and gardens or free attractions.

BE PREPARED

The prices listed in the book are regular adult, student (with ID), and kids' prices; children under the ages specified are free, but there are often ways to get a bargain. When planning your visit, always check local newspapers and family publications for coupons, special discounts, and combination tickets. Many attractions also offer discounts if you belong to an automobile club or other designated organizations. Some places even offer free admission on certain days or at certain times. When in doubt, check it out.

Call ahead to confirm prices, discounts, and hours of operation. The hours listed in this book are an attraction's basic hours, not necessarily those applicable on holidays. Also inquire about the busiest times for these attractions. When school is in session or during summer camp, lines can be long and crowds may be unbearable. On those days, consider a late afternoon visit, after the groups have headed for the buses.

Don't forget the sunscreen and hats for sunny days and outdoor locations, pocket ponchos or folding umbrellas for rain, and the portable stroller or backpack for walking distances with very young children. Be sure to pack water bottles or juice drinks to quench your thirst and a few snacks to hold the group over before your lunch or munch break. Do be mindful of those attractions that prohibit food or drink in exhibit halls or other spaces, though. Most importantly, remember this book. It easily slips into a diaper bag, beach bag, camera case, picnic tote, or purse. Don't leave home without it!

Pace yourself and your family during these excursions. There's no need to see every exhibit in the museum or every animal in the zoo. Focus on a few fun aspects of each attraction. Don't rush. If you have time for further exploration, go for it! But don't expect to cover the entire attraction in your first visit. Plan to come back, especially if this trip is a successful one for your young tourists.

It goes without saying that you should keep a close eye on your children at all times, especially if they are small. To make sure your outing is safe and successful, consider dressing your children in bright, colorful, or same-color shirts or hats. It's not a bad idea for you to do the same, so your children can spot you in a crowd. Pick a visible landmark and a meeting time to reunite just in case you become separated. When you first arrive at your destination, identify staff and security people, so everyone knows whom to ask for help or directions if needed.

I LOVE NY MORE THAN EVER

On September 11, 2001, the skyline of New York City was forever changed in a terrorist attack on the Twin Towers of the World Trade Center. Though the towers toppled, the spirit of the city soared. Countless acts of heroism, kindness, and community are witnessed daily as the city rebuilds. It is with great sadness that we mourn the lives lost on that day, but it is with great pride that we celebrate a city of strength and courage.

MAKE IT LAST

The places included and the information provided were carefully chosen to help your family create "teachable moments" and lasting memories for your children. Finding something of interest for everyone is always a challenge, but most of these places appeal to a wide age range—from toddlers to teens, parents to grandparents. To create a "teachable moment" and make a memory last a lifetime, give your child a disposable camera to capture favorite experiences on film. After your excursion, make a family adventure scrapbook or photo album. Older children may want to create a video complete with kid commentary. Handwritten journals or computer-generated diaries are also creative and fun ways to record your family fun, and these family records tend to become priceless.

Did somebody say gift shop? Yes, most of the attractions in this book have some type of retail gift boutique on the premises. To avoid a severe case of the "gimmies," save this stop for right before your go home. Before entering those portals of pricey paraphernalia, agree on the amount of the purchase and hold firm. While a small and charming souvenir can immortalize the day, there's no need to break the bank.

DON'T FORGET TO WRITE

Is there a special attraction in our countdown that your family especially enjoys? Did we overlook one of your favorite places? We'd love to hear from you. Send your e-mails to me c/o editors@fodors.com. Please include "Around New York City with Kids" in the subject line. Or drop me a line by snail mail c/o Around New York City with Kids, Fodor's Travel Publications, 280 Park Avenue, New York, NY 10017.

Wherever you go and whatever you do, have a great day. Remember you're exploring the greatest city in the world and you're traveling with the greatest kids in the world…yours.

MINDY BAILIN

AMERICAN FOLK ART MUSEUM

There's something about folk art that appeals to children. Perhaps it's the seeming simplicity, the depictions of everyday objects and creatures, or the frequent flights of whimsy. But whatever the reason, your children will probably enjoy this collection of artworks from the 18th, 19th, and 20th centuries.

Formerly known as the Museum of American Folk Art, this museum opened a new building in late 2001, while retaining its old space as a branch museum. The handsome new building quadruples the exhibition space and allows for enhanced education and programming facilities. Its inaugural exhibition season opened with American Anthem Part I, including the complete Ralph Esmerian Collection, with the familiar painting *Girl in Red Dress with Cat and Dog* by Ammi Phillips and the iconic *Statue of Liberty* weathervane. The Henry Darger Collection—26 paintings and drawings and the manuscripts of his three books—is also here.

The branch museum is primarily divided into the Daniel Cowin Permanent Collection Gallery and two changing exhibit spaces. The permanent collection highlights America's folk art

KEEP IN MIND This urban museum is special not only for the rich folk heritage of the collection it shares with the public, but also for its free admission—unusual for New York City—and its relatively late hours. The main museum's close proximity to Central Park, Carnegie Hall, shopping, and other attractions means you can make a visit here part of a fun-filled day in the heart of the Big Apple. The branch museum's convenient location directly across from Lincoln Center makes it a great spot for a pre- or post-performance cultural adventure.

Main museum: 45 W. 53rd St.; branch: 2 Lincoln Sq., Columbus Ave. and 66th St.

 212/977-7170 main museum, 212/595-9533 branch; www.folkmuseum.org

 Free; art workshop $3

 Main museum T-Th and Sa-Su 10-6, F 10-8; branch daily 11:30-7:30

 2 and up, art workshop 5 and up

heritage through paintings, sculpture, furniture, textiles, and decorative arts. Temporary exhibits spotlight a particular artist or theme. Items include dolls, carousel horses, weather vanes, and whirligigs. *Uncle Sam Riding a Bicycle*, a sculpture that moves in the wind, and the colorful *Flag Quilt* by Mary Baxter are just two examples of the patriotic art preserved here.

Guided tours, workshops, puppet shows, concerts, and storytelling take place year-round at both sites. Programs are designed in conjunction with exhibitions. Afternoon storytelling programs feature authors and artists of popular children's books, with book signings often following. Sunday afternoon art workshops (reservations required) follow guided family tours of the museums. Popular past programs have included self-portraits as animals, sock and kitchen-towel people, and 3-D comics. Children join right in.

HEY, KIDS! You might think that a city as big as New York would have new museums opening up all the time. Actually, though, this museum's new main building is the city's first new art museum built from the ground up since 1966.

EATS FOR KIDS The mezzanine level of the main museum features a small **coffee bar. The Harley-Davidson Cafe** (1370 6th Ave., tel. 212/245-6000) dishes out a bit of motorcycle memorabilia with its burgers and chili. Near the branch location, **Fiorello's Cafe** (1900 Broadway, tel. 212/595-5330) serves up mini-pizzas and, in good weather, outdoor dining. Close to Lincoln Center, the **Saloon** (1920 Broadway, tel. 212/874-1500) has an extensive menu and an occasional skating waiter.

This museum, a wonderful place of exploration, discovery, and learning for generations of children, contains over 32 million specimens and cultural artifacts. Exhibits range from dinosaurs to gems and minerals, from life in the sea to cultures from around the world to the ends of the cosmos.

A good place to begin with young visitors is the six spectacular halls containing the world's most comprehensive and scientifically important dinosaur collection. The five-story exhibit in Theodore Roosevelt Memorial Hall, featuring a *Barosaurus* rising up to protect its baby from an *Allosaurus,* is the tallest freestanding dinosaur exhibit on earth. Also making children's eyes sparkle, the Hall of Gems houses the Star of India, the world's largest and most famous blue star sapphire. The Hall of Biodiversity, which opened in 1998, features a multiscreen video projection that gives a global tour of nine ecosystems as well as a 2,500-square-foot diorama that creates a section of an African rain forest. And don't miss the replica of a 94-foot blue whale suspended in the Hall of Ocean Life. Not that you *could* miss it.

KEEP IN MIND The museum is huge, with 46 exhibition halls in 25 interconnected buildings. It's impossible to see the entire collection in one visit, so keep your focus narrow and plan to return. Each year 4.5 million people visit, so no matter when you come, you won't be alone.

HEY, KIDS! When was the last time you hunted for hidden creatures in an African baobab tree? Ever piece together the skeleton of a prehistoric *Prestosuchus* (a 14-foot reptile from the late Triassic period) in a simulated dinosaur dig? If you haven't and you're up for exploring a hands-on "museum within the museum," then head to the renovated Discovery Room. Here you can get up close and personal with some of the museum's wonders. Older kids can analyze images from the Hubble Telescope and use a seismograph to track earthquakes worldwide, on the mezzanine level. Extremely cool!

Central Park West at 79th St.

212/769-5100, 212/769-5200 museum programs and tickets, 212/769-5304 natural science center; www.amnh.org

Suggested donation $10 ages 13 and up, $6 children 2–12; museum and space show $19 ages 13 and up, $11.50 children; IMAX extra

 Su–Th 10–5:45, F–Sa 10–8:45; space shows Su–Th 10:30–5, F–Sa 10:30–8

2 and up

In 2000 the museum opened the Center for Earth and Space, a monumental 120-foot-high, 333,500-square-foot exhibition, research, and education facility, housing the renovated Hayden Planetarium. A gleaming cube of glass envelops the magnificent Hayden Sphere, some 90 feet in diameter. Here the Space Theater screens "Big Bang," an audiovisual presentation that re-creates how the universe began in a burst of radiant energy from a point smaller than a grain of sand. Though museum admission includes the Center for Earth and Space, Hayden Planetarium space shows cost extra and advance tickets are advised.

If you tire of looking at exhibits, check the IMAX movie schedule for larger-than-life films that reveal nature's wonders, shown daily on a four-story screen. Or visit the Alexander M. White Natural Science Center, which introduces children 4 and older to New York City's plant and animal life. But no matter what your game plan, call the museum in advance for information on lectures, performances, workshops, and special family events. There's just so much going on; you won't want to miss a thing.

EATS FOR KIDS Dine in the **Museum Food Court**, a state-of-the-art café offering a wide variety of food for all ages and palates. Here you'll find stone-oven pizza alongside sushi, pasta, a salad and antipasto bar, grilled sandwiches, and smoothies. The **Café on 4** overlooks the grounds at 77th Street from a windowed turret. Selections include sandwiches, salads, fruits, ice cream desserts, espresso, and cold beverages. For a burger or banana split, take a walk to **EJ's Luncheonette** (447 Amsterdam Ave., tel. 212/873–3444).

AMERICAN MUSEUM OF THE MOVING IMAGE

Lights! Camera! Action! For any fan of film or television, this museum is *the* place to see the nation's most comprehensive public collection of film and video artifacts. From Thomas Edison's Projecting Kinescope (c. 1897) to computer files used to design film sets in the 1990s, from the earliest existing television receiver (1927) to the most recent computer games, the museum has a wealth of materials from motion pictures, TV, and digital media.

The core exhibition, Behind the Screen, explores how motion pictures and TV programs are created, how they find their audiences, and how their place in our culture has evolved. Displays include such tools of the trade as cameras, microphones, and video recorders, and 13 interactive stations let you try to create a short animated movie, apply sound effects to famous movie scenes, and perform in front of a blue screen just like a TV weatherperson.

Among the collection of moving-image artifacts are costumes, posters, cameras, projectors, stage sets, fan magazines, and licensed merchandise. You can view the original Yoda puppet

KEEP IN MIND The museum offers a number of programs to enhance your visit. Movie-making exhibits are especially engaging when explained by a tour guide. Free tours are given weekdays at 3; call ahead to reserve space. Also ask about special events, such as guest speakers. Each year an array of famous film and TV actors, directors, and filmmakers make personal appearances at the museum to discuss their craft. Though these are primarily of interest to adults, some will certainly interest kids, especially teenagers. Guest speakers have included cartoonist Chuck Jones and director Spike Lee.

from *The Empire Strikes Back,* a mechanical Linda Blair from *The Exorcist,* vintage TV sets, and dolls of famous movie and TV characters, including Mr. T, Batman, Urkel, and the Simpsons. Where else can you see a gold-plated chariot from the 1959 film *Ben-Hur* alongside a collection of Fonzie paper dolls?

The museum occupies a 60,000-square-foot building across from the 13-acre Kaufman Astoria Studios complex, where *Sesame Street* is produced. Look for the address the next time Big Bird rolls the credits. Each year in the intimate 200-seat Riklis Theater, more than 300 screenings of TV programs and videotapes are presented in their original formats. Silent films are shown with live musical accompaniment. And don't pass up the neo-Egyptian Tut's Fever Movie Palace, a spoof on a 1920s theater, where hourly movie serials and shorts are screened. Since the films and videos are free, for about the cost of a movie in New York, you can have quite an experience here.

HEY, KIDS! In addition to letting you make an animated short, those interactive stations enable you to dub dialogue, create a flipbook starring yourself, or project your image onto the costumes of famous stars. You can even see how your dad would look as John Travolta in *Saturday Night Fever.*

EATS FOR KIDS You can catch a light bite in the **museum's café.** For lunch, dinner, snacks, or dessert, Broadway between 31st and 35th streets offers a large selection of restaurants and cafés within walking distance. A good choice for diner delights and Greek food, **Uncle George's** (33-19 Broadway, tel. 718/626–0593) is open 24 hours. Or follow the aroma of coffee and pastry to an outdoor table at a local pastry shop for baklava or other sweet treats.

ASPHALT GREEN

It has Manhattan's only standard Olympic-size pool, not to mention a separate teaching and exercise pool, a regulation AstroTurf field for sports, two gyms, an indoor and outdoor running track, two outdoor parks, the Mazur Theatre, and indoor and outdoor basketball courts. Whew! Are we finished yet? Not quite. Add to that a duplex fitness center, aerobics rooms, a physical-therapy/health center, and four multipurpose rooms for birthday parties and sports activities. Get the feeling it's worth visiting this campuslike, 5½-acre sports and training complex? Absolutely. And what does "asphalt" have to do with "green," anyway?

Established in 1968 where a former municipal asphalt plant once operated, Asphalt Green was created as a recreational center for city youth and the community at large. The parabolic plant building was declared a New York City landmark and today serves as a full-service sports and fitness complex. The city still owns the land, but in return for rental exemption, Asphalt Green provides a third of its services free to the community.

KEEP IN MIND Birthday party options (1½ hours, weekends only) include puppet shows, gymnastics, swimming, and other sports themes. A decorated room, paper goods, helium balloons, and a party host are provided. You supply the refreshments, guests, and, of course, the birthday child. No fuss, no mess, no bother.

HEY, KIDS! Meet Olympic swimmers, earn a medal, and get cool free stuff at the annual Big Swim. Top swimmers in each event are invited to participate in an AquaShow, featuring some of the country's best swimmers, lights, music, and a cast of 100 kids. But no matter how good a swimmer you are, if you're ages 6 to 16 you can make a big splash and help raise money for Asphalt Green's Waterproofing program, which teaches thousands of city kids to swim for free.

555 E. 90th St.

 212/369–8890;
www.asphaltgreen.org

Swim session $20 ages
17 and up, $8 children
16 and under; puppet playhouse $6 ages 2 and up

 M–F 5:30 AM–10 PM, Sa–Su 8–8;
puppet playhouse Sa–Su 10:30 and 12

 1 and up, camp
kindergarten–14

As for the "green" portion of its name, the complex also contains Dekovats and Sundial Plaza parks, which feature plenty of green space and gardens, park benches, and game tables. Dekovats adds a playground and a sprinkler during the summer, whereas Sundial Plaza has a fountain.

Children's classes are held in aquatics, sports and fitness, music, dance, and art. Offerings are varied and include swimming, diving, synchronized swimming, soccer, gymnastics, karate, and yoga. Private lessons are also available. Summer camp activities include sports and various arts: of the "fine," "performing," "crafts," and "martial" varieties. Baseball clinics, swim camps, soccer camps, and other sports minicamps run during holiday breaks.

The Lenny Suib Puppet Playhouse at Asphalt Green's Mazur Theatre stages performances with hand puppets, rod puppets, shadow puppets, marionettes, ventriloquists, magicians, storytellers, and clowns as well as exciting guest artists. About the only thing you can't do here anymore is make asphalt.

EATS FOR KIDS A popular food emporium is the **Vinegar Factory** (431 E. 91st St., tel. 212/628–9608). Come for brunch, breakfast, lunch, or dinner for fabulous sandwiches, soups, salads, and pastas. For seafood, barbecued chicken, ribs, and pork, not to mention a kids-eat-free deal every night of the week, you can't beat **Brother Jimmy's Bait Shack** (1644 3rd Ave., tel. 212/426–2020).

BROADWAY ON A BUDGET

With tickets for top shows costing up to $80 each, it can be expensive to give your family's regards to Broadway. Enter TKTS. At two locations—Duffy Square (Times Square) and Bowling Green Park Plaza—you can purchase discounted tickets to Broadway and Off-Broadway plays and musicals. (Off-Broadway is usually cheaper.) The names of available shows are posted by the booths. You probably won't get tickets to the season's smash hit—after all, they're only made available to TKTS if the theater isn't sold out—but there will undoubtedly be something that's entertaining and/or enlightening.

Lower Manhattan's TKTS booth is now located in a trailer in Bowling Green Park Plaza, opposite the National Museum of the American Indian. Lines here are shorter, and matinee tickets are sold a day in advance. The wait on the often long line at Duffy Square usually moves fast, however, and if you get your tickets here, you'll be halfway there. You can kill time around Times Square, grab a bite, and walk to the theater. Remember to bring cash or traveler's checks, because TKTS doesn't take American Express—or other credit cards.

KEEP IN MIND Most theaters are dark on Mondays, so plan your theater excursion accordingly. Scoring tickets for Tuesday through Thursday evening performances and Wednesday matinees is often easiest. If you're wondering what a show is about, where it's playing, who's in it, whether it's okay for kids, and how long it lasts, call the Broadway Line (*see above*), run by the League of American Theatres and Producers, which also sponsors the Live Broadway for Kids Club. A nifty publication, the free "Family Guide to Broadway" (tel. 800/832–8440) contains plots of the season's shows, age guidelines, schedules, prices, running times, and theater locations.

TKTS, Duffy Sq., 47th St. and Broadway; Bowling Green Park Plaza

Usually 50%–75% off regular price plus $2.50 surcharge per ticket

Duffy Sq. M–Sa 3–8, plus W and Sa 10–2, Su 11–7:30; Bowling Gr Park Pl, M–F 11–5:30, Sa 11–3:30

212/768–1818, 888/BROADWAY Broadway Line; www.livebroadway.com theater league

4 and up, but varies by show

For the best tickets, get on line early; many people arrive an hour before the booth opens. To avoid a wait, however, go later in the day, but know that many of the day's offerings may be gone. In the fall and nonholiday winter weeks, as many as 50 shows can be available, so don't despair. Family fare can usually be found. Though ticket sellers won't stop and chat about seat locations, the computer automatically lists the "best available" seats. It's likely that your family can sit together, though at the most popular shows, it may be necessary to split into twos and threes.

Another inexpensive way to see well-known long-running shows is to look for bookmark-shape discount coupons, called "twofers." They're distributed by store cash registers, near the TKTS lines, and elsewhere and enable you to buy two tickets for the price of one for selected days and times. Some theaters also sell discounted seats for unsold tickets a half hour before the curtain goes up.

HEY, KIDS! To learn more about the theater, join the Live Broadway for Kids Club, free for kids 6–18. You get a newsletter, theater discounts, info on Broadway events for kids, first dibs on tickets to Kids Night on Broadway, and other cool stuff. Call 212/764–1122 or go to www. broadway.org.

EATS FOR KIDS For sports fans and those with a craving for a good ballpark frank, score a great lunch at the **ESPN Zone** (1472 Broadway, at 42nd St., tel. 212/921–3776). For home-style cooking served family style, you can't go wrong at **Carmine's** (200 W. 44th St., between Broadway and 8th Ave., tel. 212/ 221–3800). Choose from 17 burger toppings or split a gargantuan sandwich at the **Stage Deli** (834 7th Ave., tel. 212/245–7850). Don't forget the pickles. Also see NBC Studios Backstage Tour, the New Victory Theater, Radio City Music Hall, and Rockefeller Center and the Ice Rink.

BRONX ZOO

The Bronx Zoo is the country's largest metropolitan wildlife park, home to more than 4,500 animals, including endangered and threatened species. But the exhibits here aren't fenced areas containing standard zoo animals. One example is the World of Darkness, where your children are suddenly up way past their bedtimes to get a "night view" of such nocturnal animals as leopard cats, cloud rats, and bats. They can peek at a subterranean naked mole rat colony or journey to the Himalayan Highlands to spot elusive and endangered snow leopards, fiery red pandas, and white-naped cranes.

The 265-acre zoo is too big to cover in a day and big enough to warrant returning again and again. With young children, begin in the north in parking lot B (the only year-round lot). Walk west to the Butterfly Zone and Monkey House, loop around the elephants, and land at the Children's Zoo, where learning about animals occurs by doing what animals do. Youngsters can climb a giant spider's web, try on a turtle shell, or escape like a lizard down a hollow tree, exploring five themed areas, including the one where they

HEY, KIDS!

For a bird's-eye view of the park, ride the Skyfari aerial cable car or the awesome Bengali Express monorail (May–October). Look for elephants, rhinoceroses, rare sika deer, antelope, and Siberian tigers. In summer, head to these two attractions first because lines can be long.

KEEP IN MIND Summer sees the biggest crowds, and many exhibits—the Children's Zoo, Bengali Express, Skyfari, camel rides, and Zoo Shuttle—are open only in warmer months (though the Children's Zoo is also open during Holiday Lights, mid-November through December). Not surprisingly, all those human animals, like the animals they've come to see, don't always enjoy the heat. In hot (or cold) weather, visit the indoor, temperature-controlled exhibits. Feeding times make animals active during the day. Sea lions eat at 10:30 and 3, penguins at 3:30. Or come in fall. Strollers are a must, and rentals—including those for adults—are available.

Bronx River Pkwy. and
Fordham Rd., Bronx

 718/367-1010;
www.wcs.org

 $9 ages 13 and up, $5
children 2–12, W free;
some attractions extra

 Apr–Oct, M–F 10–5, Sa–Su 10–5:30; Nov–
Mar, daily 10–4:30; Children's Zoo Apr–Oct

 1 and up, Children's
Zoo 8 and under

can pet and feed domesticated animals. If attention spans hold, walk north to the Aquatic Bird House and the Big Birds (no relation to any Sesame Street neighbors) and east past the bison before leaving.

For older children, begin in Asia Parking A (April–October), to the zoo's south. Walk to Wild Asia to experience JungleWorld, a major indoor exhibit that re-creates an Indonesian scrub forest, mangrove forest, and Southeast Asian rain forest with about 780 animals representing 99 species. Next walk northwest past the oryxes and nyalas to Africa to visit the Carter Giraffe Building before heading north to the Baboon Reserve, which re-creates the Ethiopian highland habitat of the gelada baboon. Walk west past the ostriches and storks to the newest exhibit, the Congo Gorilla Forest, a 6.5-acre indoor/outdoor African rain forest, which takes visitors into the world of endangered lowland gorillas, colorful mandrills, African rock pythons, rare okapis, red river hogs, colobus monkeys, and other spectacular species. It's a must-see.

EATS FOR KIDS **Snack stands** are located throughout the park, selling drinks, ice cream, and every other zoo snack imaginable. For more sub-stantial fare, eat at the **Asia Plaza, Terrace Café, African Market** (over-looking the Baboon Reserve), or the **Flamingo Pub.** The new **Dancing Crane Café** features a contemporary menu that includes fresh pizza, salads, sandwiches, wraps, and Italian entrées. The café can seat 210 indoors and 824 outdoors, overlooking the flamingo pond. Tables are available for those who pack a picnic.

BROOKLYN ACADEMY OF MUSIC

The Brooklyn Academy of Music (BAM), one of America's oldest performing arts centers, presents a full schedule of traditional and contemporary performing arts in the fields of dance, music, theater, musical theater, and opera. The Department of Education and Humanities offers exceptional performances for schoolchildren through the Generation BAM and kaBAM! series.

The BAMfamily series presents weekend performances for parents and children to enjoy in beautiful theaters, all at affordable prices. This great introduction to dance, music, and theater appeals to tots and teens alike. Performances are chosen to meet several criteria, including cultural diversity, multidisciplinary appeal, exposure to theatrical innovation, and the extent to which the performance is likely to introduce a young audience to art forms they may not have had the opportunity to experience before.

The Brooklyn Academy of Music also presents an annual BAMkids Film Festival, in the main

HEY, KIDS! It's time to brush up on your foreign languages. Part of the fun of the BAMkids Film Festival is watching movies from other lands. A recent festival schedule listed live-action and animated films from France, Mozambique, Brazil, Ethiopia, Mexico, Germany, Sweden, Northern Ireland, and Norway. But don't worry if you can't speak the language. Many foreign films have English subtitles, and for most of these films at the festival, the subtitles are read out loud by actors.

30 Lafayette Ave., Brooklyn

 Concerts $10

Year-round; call for schedule

718/636-4100, 718/623-2770
film festival; www.bam.org

5 and up,
film festival 4-13

building's BAM Rose Cinemas. Offerings range from animated shorts of four to seven minutes to feature films running 1½ to two hours.

Created in 1908, BAM's main building is the home of two performance spaces: the 2,000-seat Opera House and the 1,000-seat quad cineplex, the BAM Rose Cinemas. The former multipurpose Lepercq Space, also called "the black box," has been converted into the BAMcafé, a convenient spot to grab a bite in the late afternoon and evening or on matinee days. In 1987, after extensive renovation, the 900-seat historic Majestic Theater, located two blocks from the main facility, at 651 Fulton Street, opened and is now known as the BAM Harvey Theater. But whichever theater event you attend, the academy's performances will take your family on artistic journeys of memorable proportions. Bam!

EATS FOR KIDS
The **BAMcafé** (tel. 718/636–4139) opens at 4 for dinner, earlier for concessions matinee days. **Hale and Hearty Soups** (32 Court St., tel. 718/596– 5600) serves exactly that, and the 1879 landmark **Gage and Tollner** (372 Fulton St., tel. 718/875–5181) offers gaslight charm, great steaks, and seafood for special occasions.

GETTING THERE To reach BAM by car, take the Manhattan Bridge to Flatbush Avenue. Turn left onto Fulton Street and right onto Ashland Place. BAM parking is one block ahead on the right. (Hint: it's cheaper for subscribers and Friends of BAM.) If you're coming by subway, take the 1, 2, 4, 5, or Q line to Atlantic Avenue; the W, N, R, or M line to Pacific Street; or the A or C line to Lafayette Ave.

BROOKLYN BOTANIC GARDEN

It's easy to spend a day in this 52-acre blooming paradise with over 12,000 plants outside and under glass. In fact, it's easy to spend several days a year. There's something different to see each season: the Zen-like tranquillity of the Japanese Hill and Pond Garden in fall, the puffy white winter pussy willows and early bulbs bursting with color in the Rock Garden in February, a spring flowering festival of tulips, and sunny summer garden delights.

The Discovery Garden is an outdoor adventure for kids, especially preschoolers, but filled with fun for everyone. It is located immediately inside the Flatbush Avenue entrance at the south end of the garden. Your children can look through "bug-eye" lenses or blaze a trail through a bamboo forest, butterfly garden, meadow, maze, grassy areas, and a nature trail. Brightly colored Plant Discovery carts are stocked with games, puzzles, art supplies, and natural objects. (Topics and activities change regularly.) Carts also dispense free Family Fun kits for more exploration at home. Other favorite places in the botanical garden include the Fragrance Garden, where low beds are easily accessible for visitors in wheelchairs

HEY, KIDS!
Check out Amazing Plants!, a re-creation of the amazingly diverse borough of Brooklyn that'll teach you how plants survive in the city. The hands-on activities are really neat. See how seeds travel, how a plant protects itself, and just how tough urban plants can be.

KEEP IN MIND Special family events occur all year long. The fall Chili Pepper Fiesta often includes puppet shows, strolling mariachis, interactive storytelling, paper crafts, and face painting. The Cherry Blossom Festival fairly blooms with activities for children in spring, often including musical performances, martial-arts demonstrations, haiku readings, Japanese storytelling, Japanese printing workshops, doll-making, origami, and calligraphy. In addition, the garden collaborates with the Brooklyn Children's Museum (see #60) on its horticultural exhibits, including an interactive greenhouse and an exhibit titled Plants and People.

1000 Washington Ave., Brooklyn

 $3 adults, 50¢
children 6–16, T free

718/623–7200, 718/623–7220
Discovery Programs; www.bbg.org

Apr–Sept, T–F 8–6, Sa–Su 10–6;
Oct–Mar, T–F 8–4:30, Sa–Su 10–4:30

All ages

and little ones. It is the only place aside from the Discovery Garden where you're encouraged to touch the plants. Afterwards, you can rinse the smells off your fingers in a small fountain.

The Celebrity Path is paved with stones inscribed with the names of famous Brooklynites past and present. How many can you recognize? The Japanese Hill and Pond Garden is home to ducks, turtles, koi, and herons, which can be surveyed from the Viewing Pavilion. The Waiting House, shrines, bridges, and waterfalls complete a miniaturized landscape that appeals to children. A restoration of this area has resulted in better paths for strollers and wheelchairs. It's a great place for kids to see wildlife.

For a more hands-on approach, consider the drop-in Discovery Programs: Sunday workshops for 4–10 year-olds and 15-minute workshops on Tuesday for 3–6 year-olds. Sessions are held in the Discovery Garden or the Chase Manhattan Discovery Center, and topics change monthly.

EATS FOR KIDS Picnicking isn't allowed in the garden. In fact, Cherry Esplanade is the only place where sitting on the grass is even permitted. So to eat on the grounds, you'll have to go to the **Terrace Café,** which offers lunch on the Spencer Terrace April–October and in the Steinhardt Conservatory November–March. For deli sandwiches and cheesecake, take a short ride to **Junior's Restaurant** (386 Flatbush Ave., tel. 718/852–5257), a classic '50s diner. Also see the Brooklyn Museum of Art, Prospect Park, and the Prospect Park Zoo. Outside the garden's south entrance are two fast-food hamburger restaurants.

BROOKLYN CHILDREN'S MUSEUM

60

Enter through a corrugated metal tunnel lit with neon bands, and you immediately know you're on your way to an innovative, educational, fun, and fabulous place for kids. Of course, that's not how you would have entered the world's first museum for children when it was founded in 1899. Over the years, this century-old museum has served as a model for other children's museums worldwide, thanks to interactive exhibits, kids' programs, workshops, and performances.

Upon arrival, check the daily information board to see what workshops and programs are planned. Then head to any of the 10 galleries, which incorporate musical traditions, storytelling, science and nature experiments, collections, and computers to create exhibits that tickle the imaginations of young and old. On any given day, your children may be able to assemble an 8-foot-high elephant skeleton puzzle, play musical instruments from around the world, pet a snake from the live animal collection, or experiment with plants in the greenhouse. Highlights of the museum's 27,000-object permanent collection range from

KEEP IN MIND The third weekend of every month brings the Early Learner Performance Series, for children 5 and younger, and Early Learner Workshops in science, creative play, and art, from 10 to 11:30 ($5 per session). In addition, special music and dance programs are held the first weekend of every month, and free Friday Family Fun offers dance and theater performances every Friday evening during the summer.

145 Brooklyn Ave., Brooklyn

718/735-4400;
www.brooklynkids.org

Suggested donation $4

 July–Aug, M and W–Th 12–5, F 12–6:30, Sa–Su 10–5; Sept–June, W–F 2–5, Sa–Su 10–5

2 and up

masks, sculpture, instruments, and adornments from African, Central American, Asian, and Oceanic cultures to such natural history specimens as dinosaur footprints, mammoth teeth, an elephant skeleton, and a whale rib. A famous collection of dolls runs the gamut from folk dolls to a 36-piece set of Queen Elizabeth II coronation dolls designed by Madame Alexander.

Your kids can take an imaginary "walk" in over 400 shoes, featured in the exhibition Global Shoes, and can experience and explore various cultures through dance, work, and play. Visit the popular music studio, and be sure to try the "walk-on piano." Even adults can't resist. The Learning Early Gallery is dedicated to early learning for toddlers. Three theaters include an outdoor rooftop amphitheater where performances from around the world are regularly featured. You might have noticed a strong global emphasis here; along with focusing on a wealth of cultures, this place offers a world of fun.

EATS FOR KIDS
For plentiful home cooking, try the **New Prospect Cafe** (393 Flatbush Ave., tel. 718/638-2148). The **Lemongrass Grill** (61A 7th Ave., tel. 718/399-7100) is a link in a reasonably priced Thai food chain. Also see the Brooklyn Museum of Art.

HEY, KIDS! Did you know that the museum's nearly 27,000 objects and specimens have all been donated over the last century? The largest donation was from Dr. Herbert Zim, who gave 1,500 cultural objects that he collected as he traveled the world. Schools can even borrow parts of the collection as well as hands-on education kits. They're traveling exhibits that travel in a suitcase!

BROOKLYN MUSEUM OF ART

I t's the second-largest museum in New York State, established in 1823, and considered one of the premier art institutions in the world. Is it in Manhattan? No, it was born and bred—and still lives—in Brooklyn. It's the Beaux Arts–style Brooklyn Museum of Art. Over 1.5 million objects range from the art of ancient Egypt to contemporary painting and sculpture, and the museum's collections of Asian, American, Egyptian, Native American, and African art are recognized as some of the best in the world.

There are all kinds of ways to enjoy the museum with children. If you're bound for the African Galleries, pick up a "Family Guide" at the information desk to help explain what you'll see. Weekend family programs, which are free, include storytelling by guests from around the world; special dance, opera, and other music performances; and meet-the-author or -illustrator seminars. During the school year, weeklong programs are conducted for grade schoolers.

EATS FOR KIDS The **Museum Café** is open almost as long as the museum, or try the **Second Street Cafe** (see the Prospect Park Zoo). For a snack and a drink, try **Ozzie's Coffee & Tea** (57 7th Ave., tel. 718/398–6695), an interesting converted drugstore with apothecary cases.

HEY, KIDS! At the Learning Center, explore the Brooklyn Expedition (www. brooklynexpedition.org), a nifty Web site developed by this museum, the Brooklyn Children's Museum, and the Brooklyn Public Library. Containing pictures and articles about objects, exhibits, and collections plus interactive activities, it's a great resource. Once you're back at home or school—or if you can only make a virtual museum visit—you can access the site for help on projects or just for fun. Your museum experience will never end.

200 Eastern Pkwy.,
Brooklyn

 718/638-5000;
www.brooklynart.org

 Suggested donation $6 adults,
$3 students 12 and up

 W–F 10–5, Sa–Su 11–6, 1st Sa of month
11–11; Learning Center W–F 3–5, Sa 12–6

 4 and up, Arty Facts 4–7,
Gallery/Studio Program 6 and up

The Gallery/Studio Program offers students the opportunity to study the museum's diverse collections as well as work in the studio on their own art. Courses in drawing, painting, sculpture, abstract art, printmaking, collage, and mixed media are offered in 10-week sessions.

At the Learning Center, located in the first-floor Education Gallery, you and your children can browse in the museum's children's books and CD-ROMs. If you're visiting on a weekend, be sure to stop by Arty Facts (both days at 11 and 2), a new drop-in program that lets children explore the galleries, take part in a family activity, and create their own art using fun themes—all in 1½ hours. Parents of hearing-impaired children can call ahead for a schedule of sign-language-interpreted programs. As your children will discover, there's a lot more to do here than simply wander around looking at paintings, though they'll probably find that pretty special, too.

KEEP IN MIND The museum is near the Brooklyn Botanic Garden (see #61), the main branch of the Brooklyn Public Library, and Prospect Park and its zoo (see #s 16 and 15). Although you could easily spend a day at the museum, it's probably better, especially with young children, to keep your first visit short. Spend half a day here, wander to 7th Avenue for lunch at one of the restaurants or cafés, and visit another nearby destination in the afternoon. It'll break up the day and leave your children with a good memory of the museum.

CARNEGIE HALL

How do you get to Carnegie Hall? Practice...practice...or just attend one of the family concerts held throughout the year on Saturday afternoons on this world-famous stage. The family concert series, begun in 1995, introduces children to classical, jazz, and folk music at affordable, family-friendly prices. Pre-concert activities on the main stage and in other smaller Carnegie Hall spaces include storytelling, hands-on musical experiences, and instrument demonstrations. Concert-goers also receive a special "KidsBill" program specially designed for youngsters, with activities and information about each family concert.

Another wonderful concert program called Carnegie*KIDS* is designed to introduce music to preschool children. It's available to nursery schools, day care centers, kindergarten classes, Headstart programs, and small groups but is also open to families; advance registration is required for everyone. These concerts are not held in the main hall, however, but rather in the Kaplan space on the fifth floor.

KEEP IN MIND Can't get to Carnegie Hall? Let Carnegie Hall come to you! Since 1976, the Neighborhood Concert Series has hosted free one-hour community concerts in public libraries, community and senior centers, and shelters in all five New York City boroughs. A variety of artists and ensembles performing repertoires from classical and jazz to folk and pop make up each Neighborhood Concert season. Some of these concerts are Workshop Concerts or Kids Concerts. Seating is on a first-come, first-served basis.

154 W. 57th St., at 7th Ave.

  Family concerts $5; CarnegieKIDS $3; tour $6 adults, $5 students, $3 children 11 and under

 Tour M–T and Th–F 11:30, 2, and 3, performances permitting

212/247–7800, 212/903–9670 CarnegieKIDS; www.carnegiehall.org

Family concerts 3 and up, CarnegieKIDS 3–5, tour 7 and up

To make a concert experience special for children, it might help to discuss any famous musicians that you or other family members have seen perform here. Headliners have been playing Carnegie Hall since 1891, when its opening concert series included none other than Tchaikovsky conducting his own works. Since then, the hall has attracted the world's finest orchestras and solo and group performers, from Arturo Toscanini and Leonard Bernstein to Duke Ellington, Ella Fitzgerald, Judy Garland, Frank Sinatra, Bob Dylan, and the Beatles.

One-hour guided tours of the hall are also given. And if your kids want to get a close-up look at Benny Goodman's clarinet or catch a glimpse of Arturo Toscanini's baton, visit the Rose Museum, open every day except Wednesday from 11 to 4:30 or during concert intermissions. East of the main auditorium, this small museum displays an interesting array of mementos from Carnegie Hall's rich history, and admission is free.

HEY, KIDS! Movie buffs may remember that *Home Alone 2* takes place in New York City and that the lady who feeds the pigeons lives in the attic of—you guessed it— Carnegie Hall. Of course, there's no truth to the rumor that she still lives here. That's only in the movies.

EATS FOR KIDS After a concert, whistle a happy tune over to **Brooklyn Diner USA** (212 W. 57th St., tel. 212/581–8900). Go for the generous portions of kid and comfort foods or the decadent diner desserts. Keep your eyes on the fries, or try stargazing. It's a local celebrity spot. You can order a mile-high sandwich or classic cheesecake at the famous **Carnegie Deli** (854 7th Ave., tel. 212/757–2245).

CASTLE CLINTON NATIONAL MONUMENT

Like any good castle, Castle Clinton has a long history. It was built before the beginning of the War of 1812 to defend the city from sea assault, but no attack ever came. Today you can admire the views of the Statue of Liberty and Ellis Island along with the park landscape all around, while your children can enjoy looking for gun turrets and scanning the stone walls, imagining themselves soldiers defending a city.

Originally named the Southwest Battery, this circular redbrick fortress served as U.S. Army headquarters during the War of 1812. It had a timber causeway with a drawbridge connecting the fort to Manhattan and was equipped with 28 guns and a magazine inside the rounded ends of the rear wall. In 1817 it was renamed to honor the city's mayor, DeWitt Clinton. Today National Park Service rangers dressed in period costume are available to answer questions, and exhibits tell of the setting's many lives.

It's hard to imagine a more varied history. In 1824 the site was turned into an elegant entertainment facility known as Castle Garden, where the "Swedish Nightingale," Jenny

EATS FOR KIDS For dependable, kid-friendly fare, try **Houlihan's** (196 Broadway, tel. 212/240–1280) or check out the suggestions under Fraunces Tavern Museum, New York Unearthed, the South Street Seaport Museum, and the Statue of Liberty.

HEY, KIDS! How did the location and design of Castle Clinton help guard the coast of our young country? Notice that Castle Williams, on Governor's Island, is opposite Castle Clinton. Why were these two forts built so near each other? And why do you think Castle Clinton is designed in the shape of a capital D, a circle flattened on the land side? If enemy ships were moving up the East River, how could Castle Clinton help stop this attack?

Battery Park

 Free

 Daily 9–5

 212/344-7220;
www.nps.gov/cacl

 4 and up

Lind, sang in 1850. From 1855 to 1890, it served as a receiving station for more than 8 million immigrants and from 1896 to 1941 housed the New York Aquarium. Today it functions as a restored fort, museum, and ticket office for ferries to the Statue of Liberty and Ellis Island. Take a self-guided tour (20–30 minutes) or join ranger-led tours or programs (30–60 minutes). A kiosk on the parade grounds has a bookstore and information desk.

Look for the bronze statue titled *The Immigrants,* depicting a Jewish man bent in prayer with his family, along with a priest, a freed African-American slave, a worker, and a child. Paying homage to the immigrants who passed through here, it's at the beginning of a wide expanse that leads to the Netherlands Memorial Flagpole, which commemorates a different era of the site's history—the Dutch purchase of the land for Fort Amsterdam from Native Americans. Inscriptions are sculpted in English and Dutch. In all, over 300 years of history can be discovered here.

KEEP IN MIND Castle Clinton is only one of six historic National Park Service units in New York City. The others include Federal Hall National Memorial and the Theodore Roosevelt Birthplace (*see* #s 45 and 2), St. Paul's National Historic Site, General Grant National Memorial, and the Hamilton Grange National Memorial. In addition to its other functions, Castle Clinton is a visitor center for the city's national parks.

CENTRAL PARK

Central Park is to New York as the sun is to the solar system. This green oasis of over 840 acres is a magnet for families, joggers, bikers, strollers (on foot and wheels), skaters, sunbathers, and people-watchers. Where else in the city can you go horseback riding, boating, ice-skating, roller skating, folk dancing, fishing, and bird-watching; visit the zoo; and attend a play, puppet show, concert, and ball game—though probably not in one day? Weekends are busy here (but crowds make it safe), and free entertainment is everywhere. Start at the Dairy (64th St., mid-park, tel. 212/794–6564), whose exhibits and interactive videos provide an introduction. Head to 67th Street and 5th Avenue for the tree house playground. A playground at 99th Street (east side) accommodates children with disabilities. Other playgrounds are on the east side at 71st, 77th, 85th, 95th, 108th, and 110th streets and on the west side at 68th, 81st, 85th, 89th, 91st, 93rd, 96th, 100th, and 110th streets.

On land: Ride the 1903 Friedsam Memorial Carousel (Center Dr. and 65th St., tel. 212/879–0244). Belvedere Castle (79th St. Transverse, tel. 212/772–0210), home of a weather station

KEEP IN MIND It's not just couples who like horse-drawn carriage rides. Kids love them, too. You'll see the carriages assembled on Central Park South (59th Street between 5th Avenue and Avenue of the Americas) and outside Tavern on the Green. Each is decorated distinctively, and the drivers, too, are a colorful group. Some even sport top hats. Day and evening rides are available for about $34 for 20 minutes for up to four passengers. For more information, contact Central Park Carriage Rides (tel. 212/246–0520). As long as you're home by midnight, the carriage won't turn into a pumpkin and your little Cinderella will stay queen of the ball.

Bordered by 5th Ave., Central Park West, 59th St., and 110th St.

Free; some attractions charge

Daily sunrise–sunset

212/360-3444;
www.centralparknyc.org

All ages

and the Henry Luce Nature Observatory, houses nature exhibits and programs. Swedish Cottage (79th St. Transverse, tel. 212/988-9093), an 1876 schoolhouse, holds marionette performances. The North Meadow Recreation Center (97th St., mid-park, tel. 212/348-4867) has health, fitness, sports, and adventure programs, plus a climbing wall.

On or near water: At Conservatory Water (off 5th Ave. at 74th St.), children pose by literary statues. Summer storytelling takes place Saturday at 11, model boats races Saturday at 10 spring–fall. At the Charles A. Dana Discovery Center (5th Ave. and 110th St.), borrow poles and bait and head to Harlem Meer for catch-and-release fishing. To skate on frozen water, try the Wollman Memorial Rink (6th Ave. at 59th St., tel. 212/396-1010), mid-October–March (in-line skating April–September), or Lasker Rink (off Lenox Ave. and 110th St., tel. 212/534-7639)—a pool in summer. Tired yet?

HEY, KIDS! Though the park isn't even 150 years old, you can find attractions spanning several millennia. On the old side, Cleopatra's Needle, a hieroglyphic-covered obelisk east of the Great Lawn near the Metropolitan Museum of Art, dates to 1600 BC. Egypt gave it to New York City in 1881.

EATS FOR KIDS Try the **Loeb Boathouse Cafe** (see the Central Park Zoo), a seasonal open-air restaurant on the water, or a nearby cafeteria serving breakfast and lunch. For a splurge, visit famous **Tavern on the Green** (Central Park West at 67th St., tel. 212/873-3200). Twinkling lights, glitzy glass, and mirrors captivate young audiences. Pre-theater specials are reasonable, but reservations are a must.

CENTRAL PARK ZOO

By 1864, captive animals could be found in Central Park. (Of course, wild animals were here earlier, as they are today—with varying numbers of feet.) In 1934, this Animal Menagerie was remodeled, becoming the first Central Park Zoo. It was renovated again in 1980, this time by the Wildlife Conservation Society, an international conservation organization. Approximately 1,500 animals represent more than 120 species in the 6½-acre zoo, a perfect destination for little ones. It's walkable and stroller-friendly, and even the youngest tot can see the animals from low-lying or low-sitting carriages. Three climatic regions—the Rain Forest, Temperate Territory, and Polar Circle—form the focal points.

The Rain Forest is a veritable jungle, filled with the sounds and swirling mist of a roaring waterfall and the calls of tropical birds. Older children like the piranha aquarium and the ant nest, containing over 100,000 leaf-cutter ants. A way-cool sight in the Temperate Territory is an island of Japanese snow monkeys in a lake with black-neck swans.

HEY, KIDS! Did you know the sea lion pool holds 100,000 gallons of water? Check out the glass panels for below-the-water views of their swimming antics, and try to get here at 11:30, 2, or 4. That's when they're fed. It's too much fun to miss.

KEEP IN MIND Special community events like National Pig Day, Migration Sensation, and Chill Out with the Polar Bears and Penguins are scheduled throughout the year, free with general admission. An interactive preschool series for children 3–5 with an adult is offered for a fee in various sessions throughout the year. Children's and family programs (some with charges) for youngsters 6 and up have included such favorites as Breakfast with the Birds, Snooze at the Zoo, Rainforest Retreat, and Spooky Species.

Central Park at 64th St. and 5th Ave.

 212/861–6030; www.wcs.org

 $2.50 ages 13 and up, 50¢ children 3–12; some programs extra

 Apr–Oct, M–F 10–5, Sa–Su 10:30–5:30; Nov–Mar, daily 10–4:30

 All ages, children's zoo 6 and under

Speaking of cool, the Polar Circle contains some exhibits refrigerated to 34°F. Look for arctic foxes as well as the ever-popular penguins, puffins, and polar bears, whose natural habitats feature 10 viewing areas with above- and below-water views.

In the Tisch Children's Zoo, children can explore touch boxes, hear through huge rabbit ears, examine giant turtle shells and eggs, observe waterfowl from behind a child-size duck blind, and pet and feed many animals. Small animal sculptures moo, baa, or grunt when touched by little hands.

Costumed animal characters mingle with visitors, answering (and posing) questions. The Acorn Theater presents shows using puppets, costumed characters, music, and song to teach basic animal facts. Where else could you hear the "Metamorphosis Boogie" or participate in a Wildlife Workout? Something tells me it's all happening at the zoo.

EATS FOR KIDS Kids go wild for snacks at the zoo's indoor-outdoor **Cafe.** Central Park also has food stands near many entrances. You may recognize the pricey **Loeb Boathouse Cafe** (East Park Dr. and E. 72nd St., tel. 212/517–2233) from such movies as *Three Men and a Little Lady* and *When Harry Met Sally;* open March–September.

CHELSEA PIERS

Chelsea Piers has been called Manhattan's ultimate playground with spectacular views. After opening in 1995, it became the fourth-most-visited destination in the city (4.1 million visitors in 2000) in just five years, behind the Statue of Liberty and Ellis Island, the Metropolitan Museum of Art, and Madison Square Garden. This riverside recreation resort features bowling, basketball, soccer, in-line skating, swimming, sailing, kayaking, and rock climbing, and as incongruous as it sounds, your family can ice-skate in summer and play golf all winter, all on piers jutting into the Hudson River. The piers date back to 1910, part of nine piers that were a popular port of call for grand ocean liners. In 1994 the Chelsea Piers were restored and revitalized, and construction of the complex began.

The first thing to do is pick an activity. The Field House (between Piers 61 and 62, tel. 212/336–6500) is an 80,000-square-foot facility for gymnastics, team sports, basketball, soccer, and lacrosse. It contains four batting cages, dance studios, a martial arts mezzanine, and a climbing wall designed for children, teens, and adult beginners. There are open gym

KEEP IN MIND At the 1¼-mile Waterside Promenade you can stroll, grab a bench, picnic at tables, or just relax and enjoy the spectacular Hudson River views. Free summer concerts and community events take place at the tip of Pier 62 at Pier Park. But if you decide to take a walk while your kids pursue other activities (younger children, of course, should be kept with you), plan to meet up later at a specific time at an agreed-upon, no-fail place. As this recreational mecca is a vast space, without a plan, you could be pacing the piers for hours.

and open toddler gym sessions as well as open climbing. Sky Rink (Pier 61, tel. 212/336–6100) is open 24/7, if you want to ice-skate at 3 AM.

AMF Chelsea Piers Bowl (between Piers 59 and 60, tel. 212/835–BOWL) is a 40-lane facility equipped with automatic scoring, bumper bowling for kids, and Xtreme Bowling, an evening bowling experience with black lights, Day-Glo pins, music, and fog machines. A Golf Center (Pier 59, tel. 212/336–6400) houses 52 heated and weather-protected hitting stalls on four levels with a computerized automatic ball tee-up system. You and your children can practice year-round or take lessons or classes from pros.

Like the city it's in, Chelsea Piers has something for everyone—adults, kids, New Yorkers, and visitors. If you lack equipment, you can rent or buy anything you need for an extraordinary visit to this 30-acre sports village.

HEY, KIDS! Check out one of the country's best vert ramps and street courses at the recently renovated Skate Park at the Roller Rinks. Here you can safely "launch and grind" on over 20,000 square feet of ramps, pipes, flat rails, spines, fun boxes, and more.

EATS FOR KIDS Three restaurants offer on-site dining. **Rita's Burgers** (Sunset Strip at Pier 60, tel. 212/604–0441), a blend of city chic and country comfort, serves beef, turkey, tuna, and veggie burgers. **Chelsea Brewing Company** (Pier 59, tel. 212/336–6440), overlooking the marina, features casual riverside pub fare indoors or out. For breakfast, lunch, or an evening meal, try **Ruthy's Bakery & Café** (Main Plaza, Pier 62, tel. 212/336–6666). Or just picnic along the promenade.

CHILDREN'S MUSEUM OF MANHATTAN

Where do burps come from? How do you stop bleeding? Where does dead skin go? For the answers and for an unforgettable journey through the human body, visit the interactive Body Odyssey exhibit. Here you can visit a blood tunnel, where you and your children can experience the sensation of flowing through large fabricated blood vessels bathed in light. You can climb onto a giant tongue and work your way through the digestive system, shooting stomach acid and helping food churn through the intestines. Or watch as your children fight body invaders and command immune protectors in educational computer games. Geared toward youngsters 5 and up and their parents, this health and wellness exhibit is a highlight of this museum that stimulates the imagination, invites exploration, and encourages creativity and learning in fabulously fun and challenging ways.

Focusing on language development and literacy, WordPlay, for children under 4, comprises seven engaging environments designed to build cognitive, social, and physical skills. Baby Babble is a multisensory area for the very youngest visitors. Explorers' Park features

EATS FOR KIDS On weekdays, **EJ's Luncheonette** (447 Amsterdam Ave., tel. 212/873–3444) offers a 20% discount to Children's Museum of Manhattan members. For chili, burgers, and gooey desserts, sample the food at **Firehouse** (522 Columbus Ave., tel. 212/595–3139).

HEY, KIDS! If you're 6 or older, visit the Time Warner Media Center, the only production studio of its kind in the city. Here you can be part of CMOM-TV, working either on camera or behind the scenes. Techies can operate cameras, edit videos, or experiment with state-of-the-art equipment even grown-ups usually can't touch. If you'd rather be "on the air," you can read the news, do the weather with meteorologists' maps and equipment, or take part in the museum's news magazine.

Tisch Building, 212 W. 83rd St.

 $5 ages 1 and up

W–Su 10–5

 212/721–1234;
www.cmom.org

1–10

a twisting textured path for crawlers and toddlers. Apartment ABC is a child-size apartment mixing fantasy and reality, and Chatterbug Tree allows climbers to become a bird or squirrel. At the Post Office Pick-up, little ones sort letters and words and ride on the mail truck. Readers' Pond has storytelling and book-based programs, and the Resource Nook provides the latest research on early childhood education and development.

Good grief! Don't miss the Peanuts gang in a 22-activity exhibit on conflict resolution. Invention = innovation at the HP Inventor Center, where kids rethink, revise, and reshape their own design solutions using the latest technology. All inventors take home a patent application. Art classes meet in the Russell Berrie Art Studio. The Book of the Week Program takes place in the Helena Rubinstein Literacy Center. Children 18 months to 4 years can climb, slide, paint, and sing in the intimate Early Childhood Center and Creative Corner. There's always something cooking, figuratively—sometimes even literally—at CMOM. See, Mom, it's worth missing a nap.

KEEP IN MIND Sing-alongs, Step into Story Adventures, memory books to make and take, TV production workshops, and Word Wizard performances are just a few of the programs offered throughout the year. Call ahead to hear what's scheduled for the day you visit, or check the posted schedule of events as soon as you arrive. Then head first to the areas that pique your child's interest the most.

CHILDREN'S MUSEUM OF THE ARTS

It's hard to know where to begin when entering this small SoHo museum, but somehow children manage. They set their own pace, find a space that interests them, and move on, often returning to their favorite workshop or exhibit. The focus here is hands-on art, based on the theory that children learn best by doing. And they do . . . and do. In 5,000 square feet of kid-comfortable space, they touch, create, and explore.

There's always something new here, as exhibitions rotate every three months, treating such themes as art from around the world or local book illustrators. Daily workshops follow the themes of color, line, and form and always include a painting project, sculpture activity, and work using found objects, reinforcing that art can and should be made out of everything.

Your children can draw on computers and then print their work, developing computer skills, artistic sensibilities, and hand-eye coordination without even realizing it. For older kids, the Artist's Studio features daily art projects involving problem solving and exploration

HEY, KIDS! Need to shake the sillies out? Jump into the Ball Pond, a carpeted area filled with large, brightly colored physioballs. The theory behind it is that the kinesthetic experience fosters motor-skill play, but you'll probably just think that it's a great place to get started in the museum. Thanks to the creative use of color, light, and texture, the surrounding area gives the illusion of being underwater. So dive right in!

182 Lafayette St.

212/274-0986;
www.cmany.org

M–F $4 ages 1–65,
Sa–Su $5 ages 1–65

W 12–7, Th–Su 12–5

1–10, Artist's Studio 6 and over,
Creative Play Area 4 and under

with a variety of art materials. It's not unusual to find artists from the community working side-by-side with the next artistic generation here. Meanwhile, younger visitors can enjoy the Creative Play Area, which includes an Art Station, where the art projects are designed for sensory stimulation. The Art House is a small two-story space with slide shows and costumes for pretend play.

Ongoing workshops in music, dance, theater, and puppetry foster skill mastery, open-ended exploration, and creativity, instilling confidence in children. Call ahead to inquire about the times of the daily music program. Paintings, sculptures, and drawings from museum visitors, adult artists, and children from around the world are displayed in workshop areas throughout the museum. Along with changing items from the permanent collection, a number of special exhibitions and temporary displays are also hung throughout the year. Big things are created in a small space by little people with huge imaginations.

EATS FOR KIDS
In the mood for waffles any time of day? Visit the **Cupping Room Cafe** (359 W. Broadway, tel. 212/925–2898). Weekend brunch is also a treat. For a hip, moderately priced artist hangout, try **Jerry's** (101 Prince St., tel. 212/966–9464).

KEEP IN MIND The Children's Museum of the Arts conducts programs at the museum especially geared to special-needs children, their families, and schools. Another innovative series is the WEE Artists program (wondrous, experimenting, and exploring artists), held every Wednesday and Thursday morning from 10 to 11:30 for 1- to 3-year-olds. This drop-in program is a favorite with the toddler set.

CLAY PIT PONDS STATE PARK PRESERVE

New York City's only state park preserve, these 260 natural acres near Staten Island's southwest shore were once the site of a clay-mining operation (hence the name). But to really tell its history, you have to go back to the Cretaceous period, nearly 70 million years ago, when sands and clays were deposited here. More recent glacial deposits, 12,000 years ago, add to the area's geological significance. Evidence of Leni Lenape Indians, European settlers, and the Free Blacks of Sandy Ground, who arrived from Maryland in the early 1800s, adds a cultural thread to the land's rich tapestry. But though the visitor center does have historical photos and a few artifacts, the main draw here is nature.

Established in 1977, the preserve harbors such diverse habitats as fields, sandy barrens, spring-fed streams, bogs and other freshwater wetlands, and woodlands, creating an oasis amid an urban area and enabling city dwellers to commune with nature. Each season paints a different natural backdrop. Throughout the year, wildflowers or their dried silhouettes can be seen along the trails. White wild carrot flowers and Queen Anne's lace frame

KEEP IN MIND Trails are for feet or hooves only, not tires or paws. Watch for nonpoisonous snakes—garter, black racer, and water snakes—not because they'd hurt us (they won't). They're only a threat to the insect and rodent populations they keep in check.

EATS FOR KIDS There are picnic tables behind preserve headquarters. German fare is on tap at **Killmeyer's** (4254 Arthur Kill Rd., tel. 718/984–1202), and evenings often bring an oompah band. The 1716 **Old Bermuda Inn** (2512 Arthur Kill Rd., tel. 718/948–7600) is a bit pricey for lunch and dinner, but the Sunday brunch is a good value. Across from the inn is **Brick Oven Express** (2535 Arthur Kill Rd., tel. 718/967–7800), whose speciality is wood-burning brick-oven pizza and barbecue with a little pasta on the side. The center of the restaurant floor features a railroad track alongside other train decor.

83 Nielsen Ave., Staten Island

 Free; some
programs charge

 Daily sunrise–sunset,
parking lot M–Sa 9–5

 718/967–1976;
www.nysparks.state.ny.us

 2 and up

summer fields, folding up in winter to resemble tiny birds' nests. The wildflower garden behind headquarters is particularly colorful in spring, though some flowers blossom in late summer. Ask for a key to identify the garden's contents.

On your way to scope out the chicken coop, tour the weather station, or buzz around the beehives. Say hello to the two resident goats, Maggie and Mini. They love visitors and have been known to be very affectionate. Hiking and horseback riding are permitted on designated trails. Take the Abraham's Pond Trail (blue markers) to the Ellis Swamp Trail (yellow markers) for a 1-mile walk, or stay on the Abraham's Pond Trail the entire way, a ½-mile jaunt.

Free educational programming goes beyond guided and self-guided nature walks to cover pond ecology, bird-watching, tree and wildflower identification, organic gardening, and beekeeping. Campfires and children's programs round out the experience.

HEY, KIDS! Get a trail guide and look at its illustrations so you can identify the plants and animals you see on the preserve. Can you find a screech owl, box turtle, fence lizard, raccoon, or black-capped chickadee? In addition to helping put names to flora and fauna, the trail guide will alert you to landscape changes. Also look for structures, like steps or bridges, and trail markers, and remember not to disturb, destroy, or collect anything along your journey.

COLDEN CENTER FOR THE PERFORMING ARTS

Since 1961, the Colden Center for the Performing Arts at Queens College has been presenting world-class performing artists in the fields of music, dance, theater, jazz, popular entertainment, children's and family programming, and arts education. Performances can be seen at the 475-seat Irving and Susan Wallack Goldstein Theatre; the Samuel J. and Ethel LeFrak Concert Hall, a 489-seat state-of-the-art recital hall with recording studio; or the Colden Auditorium, which seats 2,127 and boasts excellent acoustics and sight lines.

KidsClassics concerts are just what they sound like: a series of classical music concerts that involve children as active listeners. An eclectic musical menu followed by a hearty serving of audience participation captivates both young and old. Before the concerts, families can create their own musical instruments and add their artwork to the portable gallery. After the concerts, audience members are invited to stay to meet the artists.

KEEP IN MIND Call the Queens College Arts Hotline (tel. 718/997–ARTS) to see what else is happening on campus. The Godwin–Ternbach Museum's collection comprises over 2,500 artworks, and four major exhibitions are mounted annually. The Queens College Art Center's Benjamin S. Rosenthal Library exhibits modern and contemporary art. The Louis Armstrong Archives contain the great jazz pioneer's recordings, instruments, manuscripts, memorabilia, photographs, and scrapbooks. The college is also working to convert his home into a museum and educational center. The Web site is another source for upcoming events; while you're there, check out the Revelations section for kids.

Queens College (off Long Island Expressway between Exits 23 and 24 at Reeves Ave.), Flushing, Queens

Varies by event

Performance times vary

718/793-8080; www.coldencenter.org

Varies by performance, KidsClassics 6–12

Family Theatre performances might include such universal favorites as the *Nutcracker* ballet, American Family Theatre's *Alice in Wonderland,* or a special musical afternoon with musician and storyteller Tom Chapin. Many events are ideal for all ages; others have age recommendations.

Besides the exceptional programming just for kids, selected all-age special events and individual performances in the fields of dance, music, and theater may also be of interest to your children. Past shows have included comedian Gallagher, 100 Years of Broadway, Dance Theatre of Harlem, Ballet Hispanico of New York, and Pops is Tops, an annual jazz concert series for children. Budding instrumentalists may also be interested in the classical concert series.

EATS FOR KIDS

For excellent, cheap noodle soup, try the Vietnamese restaurant **Pho Bang** (41-07 Kissena Blvd., tel. 718/939–5520). For cheap, fast, and hearty authentic Cantonese dishes, dine at the **Sweet-n-Tart Cafe** (136-11 38th Ave., tel. 718/661–3380).

HEY, KIDS! The KidsClassics "Classic Talk Program Guide" has really cool activities, puzzles, science experiments, and a musical "road map" to help you get the most out of these classical concerts. Rude Ralph can teach you about concert etiquette. Rap to the beat while you learn about percussion instruments and rhythm, and meet the musical members of the chamber orchestra—the instruments, that is. Try not to peek at the puzzle solutions and activity answers in the back of the book.

CONEY ISLAND

eveloped as a seaside resort in the early 19th century, Coney Island became famous as a growing amusement center in the 1880s. By the 1950s, it became less popular as a resort destination but steadily grew as a residential area. Today summer crowds still flock to the boardwalk, the 3-mile beach, a huge amusement park (Astroland), and a seaside aquarium (*see* the New York Aquarium). Fishing on the pier, go-carts, a batting cage, and a sports center offering ice-skating and indoor sports round out the recreational opportunities. On warm and sunny days, you'll find a lively mix here, with summer weekends the busiest times. Apartment dwellers come to escape the stifling summer heat; teenagers come for the thrill rides, and families flock to Coney Island with kids in tow to rekindle a memory and to create new ones for the next generation.

EATS FOR KIDS On the boardwalk, you can grab a slice of pizza, an Italian ice, a large pretzel, or, better yet, a frank. After all, this is where Nathan's Famous made Coney Island hot dog history. If you're interested in restaurants, see the New York Aquarium.

Its glory days may be gone, but Astroland Amusement Park (1000 Surf Ave.) is still a family favorite. The wooden Cyclone roller coaster remains as popular today as it was when it first ran in 1927. A water flume and 14 kiddie rides are also on the amusement menu

HEY, KIDS! Consider this. The Wonder Wheel was built in 1920 (before your grandparents were born?) with Bethlehem steel forged on-site. Standing 150 feet tall (half a football field), it has 16 swinging passenger cars and eight stationary cars and was declared a New York City landmark in 1989. The only time it stopped running was on July 13, 1977, during the infamous New York City blackout. To get the riders down to safety, the owners hand-cranked the huge wheel. Ready to ride?

Southern tip of Brooklyn

 718/855-7882 Brooklyn Tourism Council; www.brooklynX.org

 Free; Astroland and Deno's $2–$4 per ride; B&B Carousel $2.50; sideshows $3; museum 99¢

 Attractions hrs vary by season

 1 and up

here. At Deno's Wonder Wheel Amusement Park (1025 Boardwalk), 25 rides, two arcades, and an old-fashioned sweet shop are the main attractions. B&B Carousel (W. 11th St. and Surf Ave.) is also open year-round.

Lively traditional circus sideshows, complete with a fire-eater, sword swallower, snake charmer, and contortionist, are featured at Sideshows by the Seashore (W. 12th St. and Surf Ave.). Upstairs from the sideshows, you'll find the Coney Island Museum, which contains exhibits spotlighting historic Coney Island and related memorabilia. An extensive array of tourist information and literature is also available here.

Despite all its changes, Coney Island is still probably the closest you'll get to an old-fashioned seaside resort in New York.

KEEP IN MIND There are many individual (and sometimes questionable) ride operators up and down the boardwalk, so stick with Astroland, Deno's, and B&B Carousel. A real boon to the area and good news for sports fans is that baseball has returned to Brooklyn. The Brooklyn Cyclones, a minor league Class A affiliate of the New York Mets, takes to the field at the new 6,500-seat KeySpan Park (Surf Ave. between W. 16th and W. 19th Sts.). Tickets are pleasantly affordable ($6–$10) and can be ordered online at www.brooklyncyclones.com or by phone at 718/449–TIXS.

ELLIS ISLAND

A symbol of America's immigrant experience, Ellis Island welcomed some 12 million people into the United States from 1892 until 1954. Today their descendants make up almost 40% of the U.S. population, as well as many of the visitors here. Should you choose to join those millions and set foot on this landmark, you can discover or rediscover this important part of American history.

The Ellis Island Immigrant Museum tells the remarkable stories of the immigrants who passed through these buildings. In 200,000 square feet, it uses restored areas, educational facilities, and exhibits comprising over 2,000 artifacts—personal papers, jewelry, religious articles, and clothing—to tell tales of countless weary travelers. Enter through the first-floor Baggage Room, through piles of "all their worldly possessions," and view the video, which will help you plan your tour of the three-story main building and the American Immigrant Wall of Honor. (Two award-winning films are shown on the first and second floors, and an interactive learning center is accessible by reservation only.)

GETTING THERE The Circle Line ferry sails from Battery Park, South Ferry, at Manhattan's southern tip, and includes a visit to the Statue of Liberty (see #3). The trip takes 15 minutes to Liberty Island, 10 minutes from there to Ellis Island, and 10 minutes back to Battery Park. Since reservations aren't accepted, it's good to catch the first boat in the morning to avoid long lines, unavoidable during the busiest times—weekends year-round and every day in summer. Refreshments and souvenirs are sold on board. Once on Ellis Island, you can stay as long as you like—until closing time.

New York Harbor

 212/363-3200, 212/269-5755 ferry; www.nps.gov/stli

 Free; Circle Line, including Ellis Island and Statue of Liberty $7 adults, $3 children 3–17

 Daily 9–5, ferry daily every 15 or 30 min starting at 9

 8 and up

The next stop, Peopling of America, has 11 graphic displays chronicling four centuries of immigration. View the changing exhibits on the first floor before ascending to the Registry Room of the Great Hall. The hall, where immigrants were questioned and either granted or denied entry, has been restored. The cavernous space with soaring tiled arches seems to echo with the sounds of those hopeful souls.

See the remaining exhibits on the second and third floors before heading to the old kitchen and laundry building, offering a glimpse of what the island's structures looked like before restoration. Lastly, visit the American Immigrant Wall of Honor, where 600,000 immigrants' names are inscribed in steel along a promenade overlooking the Statue of Liberty. Families can pay to have a name added. Recognizable names include Miles Standish, Priscilla Alden, and Irving Berlin. It's the largest memorial wall of names in the world, fitting for a nation of immigrants.

HEY, KIDS! Most immigrants who arrived at Ellis Island were fleeing such hardships as poverty, religious persecution, and political unrest in their homelands. Do you have any ancestors who passed through the island? Try speaking to them or to someone who knows their story before your visit.

EATS FOR KIDS Pack a picnic lunch to eat at Ellis Island, or after you return, walk over to the brick plaza behind 85 Broad Street for a takeout meal from any of the area's small restaurants. Children can't go wrong at **T.G.I. Friday's** (47 Broadway, tel. 212/483–8322). Kids' meals come with balloons, crayons, stickers, and souvenir cups. Look for other nearby restaurants in Fraunces Tavern Museum, South Street Seaport Museum, and New York Unearthed.

EMPIRE STATE BUILDING

One of the most-recognized and most-photographed buildings in the world, the art deco Empire State Building has graced the New York skyline since 1931. The 1,454-foot structure with a limestone and granite exterior was built in one year and 45 days for a total of $41 million. (Renovations over the last 10 years have cost an additional $70 million, well over the original price.) Now a National Historic Landmark, it has been featured in hundreds of films viewed by millions of moviegoers. No wonder that first-time city visitors often make it their first sightseeing stop. Over 3.8 million people come here each year; the total since 1931 is over 117 million.

After you've purchased tickets on the concourse, one level below ground level, high-speed express elevators whisk you to the 86th-floor observatory in less than a minute. A temperature-controlled, glass-enclosed area offers panoramic views of the city, and you may also take in the sights from a surrounding open-air promenade. Try the on-site high-powered binoculars for a closer view.

EATS FOR KIDS Along with the observatory and gift shop, the 86th floor has a **snack bar.** The **Metro Grill** (45 W. 35th St., tel. 212/279–3535) is a great place to catch a bite to eat. Also, see restaurants in Madison Square Garden.

HEY, KIDS! Want to go for a jog? In 1978 the first annual Empire State Building Run-up was held with the help of the New York Road Runners Club. Runners ran up 1,575 steps from the lobby to the 86th floor. Today the men's record is held by Paul Crake, who ran up the stairs in 9 minutes and 37 seconds in 2000. The women's record is held by Belinda Soszyn, with a time of 12 minutes and 19 seconds set in 1996.

350 5th Ave., at 34th St.

 $9 ages 12 and up,
$4 children 5–11

 Daily 9:30 AM–12 AM, last tickets
sold 11:30

 212/736-3100; www.esbnyc.com

 2 and up

Above the observatory are broadcast and transmission facilities serving numerous FM radio stations and local TV stations. The 102nd-floor observation deck has been closed to the public due to limited capacity and long waits; it's now used only for private functions.

On your way out, pause on the 34th Street side of the building to notice the series of eight towering illuminated panels depicting the Seven Wonders of the Ancient World. In 1955 the American Society of Civil Engineers designated the building the Eighth Wonder of the Modern World. Following the September 11 attack on the World Trade Center, the Empire State Building has implemented additional security measures and has been lit from sunset to sunrise in red, white, and blue lights as a sign of hope and inspiration.

KEEP IN MIND On a clear day you can see forever—well, at least about 80 miles and to five states: New York, New Jersey, Pennsylvania, Connecticut, and Massachusetts. Needless to say, plan to visit on a sunny day. On the other hand, visiting at night has its own allure. Gazing down on the city that never sleeps reveals a sparkling tapestry. The one time you shouldn't come, however, is during inclement weather; save your money and go somewhere else.

F.A.O. SCHWARZ

It's not unusual, especially around the holidays, for lines to stream out the doors and down the sidewalk next to F.A.O. Schwarz, the world's ultimate toy store. From mid-October to the end of December an average of 75,000 shoppers a day visit this toy mecca. During December, 2.25 million people shop here, and an estimated 300,000 people per day view the 15 holiday window displays.

Embark on your own toyland fantasy as you enter this interactive store and are greeted by a toy soldier in full uniform. Look up at a giant animated clock tower that's over 20 feet tall and features dozens of moving parts, including a jack-in-the-box and a train that chugs around the timepiece. In all, three glorious floors of everything from stuffed animals to action figures, games to dolls, await the young and young at heart. Ride in the giant robot elevator for an overview of the store.

The first-floor stuffed animal collection is one of the most extensive anywhere, with many in the menagerie twice as big as your young shoppers. Remember Tom Hanks dancing on

HEY, KIDS! Have you ever dreamed of spending the night in the world's largest toy store? F.A.O. Schwarz offers a camp-out like no other in its Ultimate Saturday Night Sleep-over Adventure. Join quirky safari leaders Professors Perry Winkle and Tabitha Teazlebee for crazy crafts, a sweep through F.A.O. Schweetz (Manhattan's largest sweetshop), a dinosaur bone scavenger hunt, a romp with remote-controlled robots, a fantasy shopping spree, and a late night snack buffet. Fifteen campers, ages 6–11, receive a survival kit including customized backpack, camera, talking C-Watch, and sleeping bag. Did I mention the price tag for this extravaganza? A mere $17,500.

767 5th Ave., at 58th St.

 212/644-9400;
www.faoschwarz.com

 Free (theoretically)

 M–Sa 10–6, Su 11–6

1 and up

the giant floor keyboard in the movie *Big*? Well, it's still here, along with today's favorite computer games, video games, and blocks sold by the pound. Toys are clustered throughout the store in small boutique shops. Visit the Barbie Boutique for anything and everything under the sun for your little one's collection. Lego lovers can spend hours at the Lego Boutique, constructing the most intricate buildings and feats of engineering. Familiar favorites notwithstanding, over 70% of the merchandise here can only be found at F.A.O. Schwarz.

A free story time, held every day at 1, 3, and 5 PM, is hosted by an array of characters including Mother Goose and Geppetto, and toy demonstrators line the store, showing off the latest "must-have" toys. With all the gadgets and gizmos creeping, crawling, beeping, and zipping around the store, it's easy for you . . . I mean your kids . . . to play before you buy those new or tried-and-true toys.

EATS FOR KIDS

For scrumptious desserts, salad bar, sandwiches, and antipasto, eat at **Mangia** (50 W. 57th St., tel. 212/582–5882). For a frightfully fun meal, eat at **Jekyll & Hyde** (1409 6th Ave., tel. 212/541–9505), where special effects are more special than the cuisine.

KEEP IN MIND Compare prices beforehand, so you know by exactly how much you're overpaying. There are no great bargains to be had here price-wise, but you can't beat the selection. Browse the Web site ahead of time, and discuss spending limits. With an older child, you might even use a store visit as a lesson in basic economics. Compare prices together, and decide how best to be savvy shoppers. But since most youngsters are acquisitive as well as inquisitive, it's realistic to expect that you'll leave the store with a toy (or two) in tow.

FEDERAL HALL NATIONAL MEMORIAL

Built in 1703 to serve as New York's City Hall, Federal Hall became the first Capitol of the United States under the Constitution and is often considered the birthplace of our nation's government. On its steps stands a statue of George Washington created in 1883 by a relative of his, sculptor John Quincy Adams Ward. Washington was sworn in as the country's first president on this very site in 1789.

The original building was demolished in 1812, and the present structure was completed in 1842 and served as a U.S. Customs House. This Greek Revival building was modeled after the Parthenon, another symbol of democracy. Notice the impressive exterior's 16 Doric columns constructed of Tuckahoe marble, quarried in nearby Westchester County. Each column comprises five separate pieces, each weighing 10–12 tons. Walk through the front doors and you pass from Greece to Rome. The rotunda is based on the Pantheon and has 16 Corinthian columns.

EATS FOR KIDS Food and drink are not allowed here. **Burritoville** (20 John St., tel. 212/766–2020) serves cheap, healthy, and hefty burritos. **Cosi Sandwich Bar** (55 Broad St., tel. 212/344–5000) delights with tasty sandwiches—worth the wait. Also, see South Street Seaport Museum and New York Unearthed.

HEY, KIDS! Show me the money! When Federal Hall was a customs house (1842–62), millions in gold and silver were stored in basement vaults. No money—only exhibits—remain. Though people think of customs today mainly as a watchdog that prevents smuggling, in colonial times, it collected large fees from merchant vessels. In fact, these fees were so big that they paid for setting up the new U.S. government; creating a navy; planning and building Washington, D.C.; constructing the military academy at West Point; and reducing the national debt to zero in 1835.

26 Wall St.

 212/825-6888;
www.nps.gov/feha

 Free

 M–F 9–5

 7 and up

Begin your visit with an eight-minute animated video on the history of majestic Federal Hall, from the trial of Peter Zenger to the inauguration of George Washington. An exhibit on the Zenger trial, a milestone in the establishment of freedom of the press, also includes an antique printing press. Can you imagine printing anything longer than a page on such a primitive press? Other key events that took place in the original building include the Stamp Act Congress of 1765, meetings of the Continental Congress, the enactment of the Northwest Ordinance, the adoption of the Bill of Rights, and the first meeting of the Congress of the United States.

Models of the original structure as City Hall and exhibits about the city and the Wall Street area are interesting, too. Look for historical memorabilia such as the bible used to swear in President Washington. Free guided tours cover the history of the buildings and interpretations of memorabilia and displays. Educational programs on topics such as weapons of the American Revolution are conducted at 12:30, 2, and 3:30. It's like a social studies textbook come to life.

KEEP IN MIND In addition to finding information at Federal Hall about the site itself, you can also obtain brochures with self-guided themed walking tours of Lower Manhattan. While you're in the area, check out Castle Clinton, Fraunces Tavern Museum, Ellis Island, the Statue of Liberty, the National Museum of the American Indian (*see listings*), and the Staten Island Ferry. By talking to a park ranger here, kids can take part in the Junior Ranger program and get a packet of goodies including a Junior Ranger badge.

FORBES MAGAZINE GALLERIES

The Forbes Magazine Galleries showcase changing exhibitions from the magazine's collection of paintings, photographs, and autographs, but the big draw for kids is the personal collection of the late publisher Malcolm Forbes, on the ground floor, which includes toys and games and other unusual and sparkling items.

Items in the Toy Galleries include over 500 toy boats and an army of 10,000 toy soldiers engaged in imaginative displays. A special concave viewing window lets children enter the whimsical childhood room depicted in Robert Louis Stevenson's poem, "The Land of Counterpane." Also ongoing here is a display of original handcrafted versions of the board game Monopoly and the game that inspired it, the Landlord's Game. A 1913 English version called the Br'er Fox an' Br'er Rabbit game is also exhibited. But Forbes's noted collection goes far beyond toys to include historical documents and memorabilia. Thomas Jefferson's bottle of 1787 Château Lafite, Abraham Lincoln's stovepipe hat, and various presidential papers reveal the personalities and problems of many U.S. presidents. Four miniature

KEEP IN MIND For children (and adults) truly smitten by what they see, here are a few publications to check out: *Forbes Galleries* covers collection highlights and has an introduction from the collector himself. *A Lifetime of Collecting* is Forbes's autobiography, containing 572 photographs showcasing many of his treasures. *Toy Boats* offers a pictorial history of the rare tin, cast-iron, and wooden boats, dating from 1870 to 1955, in the Forbes collection.

Forbes Building,
62 5th Ave., at 12th St.

 Free

 T–W and F–Sa 10–4,
Th group tour only

 212/206–5548

 4 and up

rooms—Washington's headquarters at the Battle of Yorktown, John Adams's kitchen law office in Massachusetts, Ulysses S. Grant's dining room, and Jefferson's bedroom and study at Monticello—forge snapshots of American history.

If your youngsters find history dull, they might find the trophies, medals, and awards in the Mortality of Immortality exhibit shinier and more interesting. As Forbes wrote, "The trophy memorabilia are humbling reminders that objects marking great occasions or victories cannot stop the march of time and that, as the pharaohs learned, you can't take the stuff with you." Even more likely to catch the young gallery visitor's eye are 12 of the fabled Easter eggs made by the House of Fabergé for the last two Russian czars, along with over 400 other treasures made under the direction of master jeweler/goldsmith Peter Carl Fabergé. The collection can't help but make you think that, wealth and power notwithstanding, Forbes had a lot of kid in him.

HEY, KIDS! Do you collect anything? When did you start? Don't worry if your collection is a little smaller than Forbes's; he had a whole lifetime and a lot of money to spend. To have even more fun, visit the library to learn more about your treasures and how to catalog them.

EATS FOR KIDS In the mood for comfort food? Try **America** (9 E. 18th St., tel. 212/505–2110). For big, big, big burritos at low, low, low prices, try **Benny's Burritos** (113 Greenwich Ave., tel. 212/727–0584). **NoHo Star** (330 Lafayette St., tel. 212/925–0070) offers American as well as Chinese fare. Children will probably opt for hamburgers and french fries, omelets, or pancakes, while parents can be a bit more adventurous.

FRAUNCES TAVERN MUSEUM

The fact that this museum is open on July 4 and Washington's birthday (though closed on other holidays) should immediately tell you something about it. Fraunces Tavern—a large brick house built by Etienne Delancey in 1719 on the city's first landfill—was a meeting place for the Sons of Liberty as well as the site where George Washington said farewell to his loyal officers at the Revolution's end. Today it serves as a museum of early American history and culture, a survivor of the early days of New York City.

The building got its name from tavern-keeper Samuel Fraunces, who ran one of the finest dining and drinking establishments in colonial New York. Colonial governor George Clinton threw a huge gala here on Evacuation Day, when the last British soldiers left American soil. The tavern building was also where the Departments of War, State, and Treasury were housed when New York was the first capital of the United States.

HEY KIDS! Don't miss the daily tours that give a kid's-eye view of Colonial times. These journeys to the past include lots of hands-on fun and interactive games just for kids 12 and under.

KEEP IN MIND Walking tours and Colonial Tea Parties are just some of the public programs held at the Fraunces Tavern Museum that can enrich your museum experience. But it's a good idea to call the museum's recorded information line ahead of time to determine which of the upcoming programs are appropriate for the ages in your family.

54 Pearl St.

 212/425–1778

 $3 adults, $2 students 7 and up; some special events extra

 M–F 10–4:45, Sa–Su 12–4

 6 and up

Start at the Visitor Orientation Exhibition, which illustrates the history of the tavern and early New York. From there, visit the Long Room, site of Washington's famous farewell address and now a re-created 18th-century public tavern room. The Clinton Room, named for George Clinton, the first American-born governor of New York, represents an early 19th-century private dining room. A Flash of Color: Early American Flags and Standards highlights national symbols from different periods throughout American history. Included are regimental flags from the Revolution, flags of French troops, and naval banners. Changing exhibitions also shed light on Colonial times.

Summer Sundays welcome you to participate in special events, like tavern games, candle-making, and ice cream socials, for a modest fee. Reservations are recommended. And on those special holidays—Washington's Birthday and Independence Day—Fraunces Tavern Museum holds open houses where you may pay as you wish to partake in the day's festivities.

EATS FOR KIDS It's more expensive than the neighborhood's many delis, coffee shops, and sandwich places, but if you want to go back in time, dine at the completely renovated **Fraunces Tavern** (tel. 212/968–1776), part of the complex that includes the museum. It's good for pot roast, and though there's no children's menu, young diners can be accommodated with sandwiches, pasta, or similar fare. (Like many of the area's restaurants catering to a Wall Street crowd, the tavern is closed on weekends.) Also see eateries in the South Street Seaport Museum and New York Unearthed listings.

HISTORIC RICHMOND TOWN

In the heart of Staten Island, this beautiful 100-acre park may be one of the city's best-kept secrets. The village contains 28 preserved historic buildings and a few reconstructions that interpret three centuries of Staten Island's daily life and culture. Ten buildings are on their original sites; the others were moved from elsewhere on Staten Island.

The village of Richmond began in the 1690s as a crossroads settlement among scattered farms. The Congregation of the Reformed Dutch Church built a combined religious meeting house, school, and residence for its lay minister and teacher around 1695. By 1730, Richmond had become the island's principal political center, and throughout the 18th century, the village continued to increase in importance, acquiring a jail, courthouse, churches, taverns, and shops. By the early 19th century it had become a popular retreat for city residents.

Few barricades separate visitors from the places where people once worked and lived. Each room, whether equipped with the tools of a trade or filled with the aroma of something

KEEP IN MIND If you're planning a visit, call to see if any special family events (reservations required for some) are coming up. A sampling includes Halloween in Richmond Town, Old Home Day, Christmas in Richmond Town, a Victorian Ball, an Independence Day Celebration, Pumpkin Picking at the Decker Farm, a historic military Encampment Weekend, and a Victorian Valentine Party. The Richmond County Fair also takes place here, combining traditional events with modern pastimes.

441 Clarke Ave., Staten Island

 July–Aug, W–F 10–5, Sa–Su 1–5;
Sept–June, W–Su 1–5

$4 adults, $2.50 children
6–18 and students; some
special events extra

718/351–1611;
www.historicrichmondtown.org

3 and up

baking, will take you back in time. Begin at the 1837 Third County Courthouse Visitor Center to get a visitor's guide to points of interest. The Historical Museum is in the former County Clerk's Office. The Voorlezer's House is Richmond's oldest building on its original site as well as the country's oldest elementary schoolhouse. A one-room grocery store from Eltingville now depicts an 1860 printing shop. Your children will chuckle at the outhouse and marvel at demonstrations of printing, tinsmithing, and other trades performed by artisans in period costumes. When demonstrations aren't happening, a guide is present to give an overview of the setting and answer questions.

Special events are offered at various times, but you can count on traditional folk and ethnic music—showcased in the Tavern Concert Series—on Saturday evenings, January–April. The 19th-century Guyon Tavern is warmed by a woodstove and lit by candles to add to the atmosphere.

HEY, KIDS! More than 200 of the best-loved toys from the 1840s to the present are displayed in the Historical Museum. Can you recognize the toys and how children played with them? Imagine what childhood, family life, and work were like in the days of those toys.

EATS FOR KIDS The Parsonage (74 Arthur Kill Rd., tel. 718/351–7879) serves some history with your meal. It was the official residence of the Reformed Dutch Church minister (1855–1875). **M. Bennett Refreshments** is in the former cellar bakery in the Greek Revival–style Bennett House. The popular summertime traditional dinner, held once a year, includes an Early American menu prepared over open fires with music, games, and century-old toasts (reservations required). A picnic area is just east of the visitor center.

INTREPID SEA AIR SPACE MUSEUM

41

Not your typical museum, the Intrepid Sea Air Space Museum is a unique part of the landscape—make that seascape—of Manhattan's west side. The U.S.S. *Intrepid*, a 40,000-ton, 900-foot-long aircraft carrier, launched in 1943, was once scheduled to be scrapped after 31 years of military service. However, in 1982, after a successful campaign to save it, this historic ship was put into different service—as a museum.

Your children don't have to know history to sense adventure when standing among dozens of vintage and modern aircraft parked wing to wing on the carrier's flight deck, or when hearing a former crew member tell stories of this noble vessel. Video kiosks display the ship's heroic past, which includes five kamikaze strikes, one torpedo attack, and seven bombs. After each repair, the ship returned to active duty, earning her a reputation as the "Ghost Ship."

HEY, KIDS!
Fly your own jet mission aboard a navy flight simulator in Desert Storm Strike. Take off in your F-18 Hornet jet fighter. Dodge enemy tanks, missiles, and hostile aircraft as you attempt to return unharmed. Admission is $5 in addition to museum entry.

EATS FOR KIDS When was the last time you dined on a 900-foot-long aircraft carrier? The crew's mess has been refurbished so you can eat your meals here, just like the crew did. Bring your own if you like. A variety of sandwiches, snacks, and drinks can also be purchased on board. A new **McDonald's** has opened in the new Visitor's Center area, near the gift shop.

Pier 86, W. 46th St. and 12th Ave.

 212/245-0072;
www.intrepidmuseum.org

 $12 adults, $9 students
12 and up, $6 youths
6–11, $2 children 2–5

 Apr–Sept, M–F 10–7, Sa–Su 10–6;
Oct–Mar, T–Su 10–5

 3 and up, U.S.S.
Growler 6 and up

But there are other craft here, too. You can take a guided tour of the U.S.S. *Edson,* from its impressive engine room to its mess decks. The 418-foot Vietnam-era naval destroyer is the most thoroughly restored vessel here. Don't miss the U.S.S. *Growler,* the only intact strategic missile submarine open to the public. Since 1989, this 3,000-ton, 317-foot-long sub has offered a firsthand look at life on board as well as the once "top-secret" command post. And you can tour the Lockheed A-12 Blackbird, the world's ultimate spy plane. Along with the Blackbird, the *Intrepid*'s aircraft collection includes WWII fighters, supersonic jets, wood and canvas biplanes, and an F-16 Air Force Falcon, just to name a few.

Also here is Felix DeWeldon's original sculpture of the Iwo Jima Memorial, which portrays five marines and a sailor raising a U.S. flag during WWII. (The more famous, larger version is on display at Arlington National Cemetery.) Like the rest of the exhibits at this museum, it's a tribute to the people and vessels who have served our country at sea.

KEEP IN MIND Prepare your kids ahead of time for the possible wait to tour the U.S.S. *Growler.* Access is limited to only 15 people at a time, and very young children are not allowed aboard. And, if you have a friend or relative who served or serves aboard ship, you might want to bring him or her along; someone with firsthand experiences can certainly enhance your children's experience of this museum.

JEWISH MUSEUM

Nestled in the elegant 1908 Warburg Mansion on the city's Museum Mile, the Jewish Museum chronicles 4,000 years of history and culture through art. The permanent exhibition, called "Culture and Continuity, the Jewish Journey," occupies 17 galleries on the third and (completely renovated) fourth floors. A new family audio guide (free), for ages 5 and up, and a new activity book ($18 in the museum's shop) guide you through this core exhibit. Art, artifacts, and media installations examine both perpetual and changing aspects of the Jewish cultural experience. Young visitors tend to find the re-creation of an ancient synagogue of interest, whereas older children enjoy television and radio programs from the museum's broadcast archive as well as a film on Jewish rituals in a gallery filled with ceremonial objects.

In addition, many areas and programs at the Jewish Museum are specifically devoted to children. The fourth-floor Children's Gallery has changing exhibitions for young visitors, and each always includes interactive components for inquiring minds and busy hands. On

KEEP IN MIND If your family finds it hard to come up with something to do on Christmas, consider coming here. Unless December 25 falls on a Saturday, the museum hosts a special Family Day with a huge array of family activities, including a colossal art workshop in the auditorium, live music, and children's video screenings. How many museums do you know of that are open on Christmas?

1109 5th Ave., at 92nd St.

 212/423-3230;
www.thejewishmuseum.org

 $8 adults, $5.50 students
13 and up; T after 5 free

 Su-M and W-Th 11-5:45,
T 11-8; Family Activity Center
Su 1-4; story time Su 1:30

 2 and up

Sunday, you can drop into the Family Activity Center and participate in a hands-on crafts workshop for a nominal materials fee; you can also listen to a free ½-hour story time or take part in free Children's Gallery talks, informal interactive minitours of the core exhibit that meet on the third floor. The museum's first two floors contain temporary exhibits that are more often of interest to adults, and there are two gift shops, one in the museum and one next door in a brownstone.

Other family programs include Children's Film Days, in which films are often followed by art workshops related to the movie shown; Stories and Songs for Tots; Art in the Afternoon; and holiday craft and activity workshops. Many events are free; others have a small fee. Family concerts and special performances by well-known artists, like Marc Weiner from *Weinerville,* are scheduled throughout the year. Just check with the museum by phone or on its Web site to see if something's happening that would interest your family.

HEY, KIDS! Look for Ari (that means "lion" in Hebrew) throughout the museum and on the Web site. Ari's picture marks fun, family-friendly experiences. And don't forget to say "shalom," which means "hello" and "good-bye" as well as "peace" in Hebrew.

EATS FOR KIDS Lunch, snacks, and a light dinner are available at the museum's **Cafe Weissman.** You can't go wrong at the **Barking Dog Luncheonette** (1678 3rd Ave., tel. 212/831-1800), offering breakfast, lunch, dinner, brunch, and a drinking fountain just for canines, in case you've brought your pooch (though naturally it won't be allowed inside). For homestyle, wholesome food, not to mention a great Sunday brunch, try **Sarabeth's** (Hotel Wales, 1295 Madison Ave., tel. 212/410-7335).

JONES BEACH STATE PARK

New York State's most renowned state park opened in 1929 and hosted 1½ million visitors its first year. Sunday traffic jams on the (then) Wantagh Causeway started soon after, and not much has changed since. Today, the Wantagh Parkway still jams up on weekends as families flock to the beach's eight Atlantic Ocean bathing areas and Zachs Bay from points even farther than New York City, 33 miles away.

The park comprises 2,413 acres with 6½ miles of beach frontage and ½ mile of bay frontage. East and West bathhouses feature Olympic-size pools, diving areas, wading pools, lockers, and showers. A 2-mile boardwalk is popular with young and old, and there are shuffleboard courts, paddle tennis, softball fields, volleyball, miniature golf, a fitness course, basketball, dancing nightly at the band shell, concerts, and special events.

Surfing is permitted at the West End 2 area from the Monday after Thanksgiving through Labor Day, so surfer-free families may wish to avoid this crowd. With really young children,

GETTING THERE

By train, take the LIRR to Freeport or Wantagh, where buses (tel. 212/526-0900) connect to the beach. Recreations Lines (tel. 718/788-8000) runs buses from Manhattan. By car, take the Northern or Southern state parkways or LIE east to the Meadowbrook or Wantagh parkways south to the park.

EATS FOR KIDS

Part of the fun of the beach is crunching that sand in your peanut butter sandwich. But for those who choose not to cart a 10-ton cooler across the beach, refreshment stands dispense drinks, cool desserts, hot dogs, and snacks. Barbecue and picnic areas are also abundant. The **Boardwalk Restaurant and Terrace** (Central Mall, tel. 516/785-2840) features lunch, dinner, and Sunday brunch. The **Seaside Sweet Shoppe** (West Bathhouse), modeled on an old-fashioned ice-cream parlor, has table and counter service.

head to Zachs Bay, a gentle bathing area (don't even think about waves). Moms and dads have been dutifully depositing tots 10 yards from the family blanket in a puddle of water for years, and it's still a great first ocean experience.

The Jones Beach Theatre, at Zachs Bay, offers a sensational summer concert schedule with seating for 14,000. A 104-foot-wide stage with a 76-foot revolving center has an underwater tunnel leading from shore to stage and underground elevators for supplies and scenery. Though most shows are geared for adult and teenage audiences, some concerts will interest families with youngsters.

Surf fishing areas, docks, a boat basin, and bait station make for good fishing, and the new Theodore Roosevelt Nature Center (West End 1) gives your family something to do when it rains. Whether you want to play, sunbathe, or swim, Jones Beach is ideal. Too bad so many people know it!

HEY, KIDS! As you approach the beach by bus or by car, be on the lookout for the Jones Beach Tower, a familiar landmark modeled after the campanile of St. Mark's Cathedral in Venice. It's 231 feet high and made of brick and stone, housing a 315,000-gallon water tank. Believe it or not, this tower provides all the water for the entire park. So if you're about to ask, "Are we there yet?" just look for the Jones Beach Tower instead.

LIBERTY SCIENCE CENTER

Many consider this one of the nation's top 10 science centers. The first thing to wow your children (and you) is the 700-pound Hoberman Sphere, which expands and contracts repeatedly in the atrium. It's mesmerizing to watch it seemingly explode into the huge space. But don't linger too long, or you'll miss all the fun on the three themed floors.

On the Environment Floor, you can climb across a 20-foot rock wall full of fossils or take a close look at sea urchins and spider crabs in the Touch Tank. Get your hands dirty at the Stream Table before making friends with insects, snakes, and reptiles in the Green House Discovery Room.

A popular Health Floor destination for the 7-and-up crowd is the Touch Tunnel. Crawl through this 100-foot black tube with only touch to guide you. Close by, enter the world of optical illusion in the Perception Maze. At the medical imaging station, you can use MRI and CT scans to explore the human body, and don't forget to climb into the ambulance.

GETTING THERE Don't let the New Jersey location scare you; driving takes under 30 minutes. Just get to New Jersey Turnpike exit 14B, bear left after the tollbooth, and follow signs. Or take the PATH to the Exchange Place or Pavonia/Newport station, where you can transfer to the sleek new Hudson–Bergen Light Rail for a 15-minute ride to Liberty State Park. Then follow the science experiments embedded in the sidewalk to the center. You can also take the NY Waterway ferry (*see #18*) from the World Financial Center to Jersey City's Colgate Center and take a bus (call 201/432–8048 for schedules).

Liberty State Park,
Jersey City, NJ

201/200–1000;
www.lsc.org

$9.50 adults, $7.50 children 2–
18; IMAX and laser show extra;
July 4 all 3 free

Apr–Labor Day, daily 9:30–5:30;
early Sept–Mar, T–Su 9:30–5:30

2 and up

Next comes the Invention Floor. At the Chromakey stage, use the magic of video to put people on the moon or in a jungle. Challenge a computer in the virtual sports stadium to basketball, Ping-Pong, or soccer. At the USAF Flight Simulator, navigate a plane over a 100-mile radius from the science center, passing many New York landmarks.

Each exhibit floor has a discovery room, where staff members present hands-on activities, and a science demonstration stage, where informative and entertaining shows take place. Don't miss a 3-D laser journey in the Joseph D. Williams Science Theater or the latest IMAX film on the IMAX Dome Theater's six-story screen. Many of the over 250 participatory exhibits may be too complex for preschoolers, but each floor has some activities for them. Each year brings six or so traveling hands-on science exhibitions, and since its 1993 opening, over 6 million people have visited. Is it any wonder?

HEY, KIDS! At the science center's Web site, you can meet Betty Bug–a.k.a. Dr. Betty Faber, staff scientist and entomologist. She'll show you some cool stuff to see and do. It's the "creepiest" Web site you'll ever log on to.

EATS FOR KIDS Check out the **Laser Lights Cafe,** on the main floor, for reasonably priced entrées that appeal to both young and old. Choose from pizza, burgers and fries, franks, chili with cheese, sandwiches, and salads. This cafeteria makes for a nice break in a full day and a good place to plan your strategy for the afternoon.

LOWER EAST SIDE TENEMENT MUSEUM

37

Chronicling a variety of immigrant and migrant experiences in Manhattan's Lower East Side, this urban living-history experience comprises a series of guided tours of an 1863 tenement building (the first tenement declared a National Historic Landmark) and its neighborhood. Free video presentations tell the history of the building and neighborhood, and feature interviews with residents past and present.

The three tours start at the Visitors Center. "Walk the Streets Where We Lived" is a one-hour stroll through the Lower East Side, including public spaces and historic buildings, such as the old Jewish *Daily Forward* Building on East Broadway (April–December, weekends at 1 and 2:30). This tour is probably too much for young children. A better choice is the 45-minute "Confino Family Apartment" tour, which focuses on the Sephardic-Jewish Confino family in 1916. It runs hourly on weekends 12–3. "Tour a 19th Century Tenement" is an hour-long visit to the apartments of the Gumpertz family from Germany, the Rogarshevsky family of Lithuania, and the Baldizzi family from Italy. A look at an

EATS FOR KIDS
Ethnic eateries abound. Have a knish or potato latkes (pancakes) at **Yonah Schimmel's Knishery** (137 E. Houston St., tel. 212/477–2858), a Lower East Side institution that began from a pushcart. For dim sum or veggie dumplings, try **20 Mott Street** (20 Mott St., tel. 212/964–0380).

HEY, KIDS! The 45-minute tour of the Confino family's apartment is specially designed as a hands-on experience. You will be met by a costumed guide who will welcome you as if you are an immigrant just arrived in the neighborhood. Try on period clothing. Ask Mom and Dad to show you how to fox trot to the music on the authentic wind-up Victrola. If you try hard enough, you just might be able to imagine a child's life here in 1916.

Visitors Center, 90 Orchard St., at Broome St.; tenement, 97 Orchard St.

 212/431-0233; www.tenement.org

 1 tour $9 adults, $7 students; multitour discounts

 Visitors Center daily 11–5:30; tours vary

 8–16

unrestored apartment is also part of this tour, as is a holiday season glimpse of the Gumpertz and Baldizzi families' observance of Hanukkah and Christmas. These are conducted Tuesday–Friday 1–4, every half hour, weekends 11–4:30, every 20 minutes.

Round-table discussions on mostly adult topics are scheduled year-round as are children's and family programs. The Tenement Theatre at John Schneider's Saloon, in the tenement's basement, stages plays and vaudeville acts relating to Lower East Side history.

If you have a relative or friend who was an immigrant on the Lower East Side, or who knows stories of those days, you might want to invite that person along to provide a first- or second-hand perspective. Or take a decidedly more modern (virtual) tour by logging onto the museum's Web site. However you visit, your children will probably gain an appreciation for New York's present by catching a glimpse of its past.

KEEP IN MIND Tickets for all tours are available at the Visitors Center on a first-come, first-served basis, and they sell out quickly, as groups are limited to 15. In addition, tickets for weekday tours and programs may be purchased in advance by credit card by calling 800/965–4827 or through the ticket Web site at www.ticketweb.com. Sundays at the museum are especially crowded, but if you come by car, you can enjoy four hours of free parking at a lot on Broome Street, between Norfolk and Suffolk streets, courtesy of the Historic Orchard Street Shopping District.

MADAME TUSSAUD'S WAX MUSEUM

Leave your autograph book at home, but grab your camera and get up close and personal with your favorite celebrities at Madame Tussaud's Wax Museum. Though Madame Tussaud's has been entertaining Europeans with its signature wax portraits for more than 200 years, this $50 million, 85,000-square-foot, five-story showplace is new. Nearly 200 uncannily lifelike wax portraits are featured in six themed, interactive exhibits. You can take photographs of your family with a virtual who's who of movies, music, sports, and television, as well as world leaders and other influential historical personalities.

The Opening Night Party, in a baroque Italian garden, lets you mingle with the New York A-list while waiting for the latest Broadway reviews to be posted. Look for Samuel L. Jackson, John Travolta, Oprah Winfrey, Hugh Grant, Bette Midler, Meryl Streep, and Nicolas Cage, among others, sharing the latest gossip. Go Behind the Scenes, with Al Roker, uses multimedia displays to demonstrate the often painstaking methods used to create a wax portrait. Follow Roker from his first sitting to the final touch-up of hair and make-up.

KEEP IN MIND If you have young or extremely sensitive children, do not—repeat, do not—enter Madame Tussaud's Story, which follows the Opening Night Party. In an 18th-century setting, the exhibit chronicles the 200-year history of Madame Tussaud and her work and depicts scenes from the French Revolution as well as the beheading of Marie Antoinette and Napoleon's lover Josephine in prison. The disturbingly graphic display, sounds of war, and dark, depressing scenery are extremely alarming to youngsters. (Trust me on this one.) To bypass the room, simply look for the adjacent door marked for the Behind the Scenes area.

In the Gallery you'll come face-to-face with American presidents and great leaders who've made a difference. Can you find the Dalai Lama, Maya Angelou, John F. Kennedy, Albert Einstein, Martin Luther King, Jr., and Diana, Princess of Wales? Move on to Popular Culture, where you'll meet trendsetters and celebrities. Babe Ruth, the Beatles, Marilyn Monroe, Neil Armstrong, Bill Gates, and Frank Sinatra are all presented in decade-specific vignettes.

The "combined experience," costing slightly more than the museum alone, admits you to It Happened in New York, a magical midnight ride via virtual Hansom cab through major events in New York City's illustrious history. Young children (and some adults) may find it a bit uncomfortable to look up at the domed ceiling screen while leaning on rails (no seats here). Is it any wonder that nearly 12 million guests visit Madame Tussaud's sites around the world each year?

HEY, KIDS! It takes six months to create a wax figure, including five weeks alone for each head, since hair strands are inserted individually. Once on exhibit, each wax portrait is inspected and groomed daily, and its hair is washed and makeup retouched regularly.

EATS FOR KIDS Directly across the street, **Chevys** (259 W. 42nd St., tel. 212/302–4010) has great Tex-Mex food and an extensive menu for kids and adults that's not a lot of dough. Speaking of which, the kids' crayons come in a mound of dough, which isn't how Madame Tussaud got her start in sculpting. In the same building but two doors down from the Wax Museum, the **42nd Street Eatery** is a food court with a **California Pizza Kitchen, Applebee's, Chili's, Ranch 1,** and **Cinnabon.** If you can't find something to eat here, go home for lunch.

MADISON SQUARE GARDEN

35

Sitting on top of Penn Station and spanning nearly 1 million square feet in the heart of New York City, this is perhaps the world's most famous arena. Generations of New Yorkers can fondly remember coming to various incarnations of "the Garden" to see a variety of sports, from boxing to basketball, as well as other types of performances. Today's Madison Square Garden traces its beginnings to the 1874 Great Roman Hippodrome, built by showman P.T. Barnum. In 1877 it was taken over by bandmaster Patrick Gilmore and renamed Gilmore's Garden. In 1879 Cornelius Vanderbilt's son, William, renamed the complex Madison Square Garden, and so its descendant—which opened in 1968 and was fully renovated in 1991—is known today.

The main arena seats 20,000 and is the spring site of performances by Ringling Bros. and Barnum & Bailey Circus. It is also home to the New York Knicks and New York Liberty basketball teams, New York Rangers hockey team, and events ranging from tennis tournaments to boxing bouts, and from horse shows to track meets. In 1877 Gilmore's Garden played

HEY, KIDS! The Walk of Fame showcases names—from Elton John to Billie Jean King to Gunther Gebel-Williams—representing over a century of memorable sports and entertainment. In 1992 the first 25 members, chosen from over 240 nominees, were inducted. See how many famous people you can identify.

EATS FOR KIDS You can get a deli sandwich at **Ben's Kosher Delicatessen** (209 W. 38th St., tel. 212/398–2367) or dunk a donut at **Krispy Kreme** (2 Penn Plaza, 33rd St. on Amtrak level, tel. 212/947–7175). Head to Macy's Herald Square and **Emack & Bolio's** (151 W. 34th St., 4th floor, tel. 212/494–5853) for creamy ice cream and yogurt in heavenly flavors. In addition to providing Garden memorabilia discounts, your tour ticket stub is good for 10% off lunch in the Garden sports restaurant, **Play by Play** (4 Penn Plaza, tel. 212/465–5888), weekdays 11:30–2:30. For other choices, check out Penn Station's lower concourse.

7th Ave. between 31st and 33rd Sts.

 Events vary; tour $13 ages 13 and up, $11 children 12 and under

 Event times vary; tour M–S 10–3, Su 11–3 every hr

212/465–MSG1, 212/465–5800 tours; www.thegarden.com

 Varies by event; tour 7 and up

host to the first annual N.Y. Bench Show, now famous as the Westminster Kennel Club Dog Show. Various ice shows and other children's fare are offered throughout the year. The 5,600-seat Paramount Theater, today known as the Theater at Madison Square Garden, also hosts children's shows, such as *Sesame Street Live, The Wizard of Oz,* and *A Christmas Carol.*

Your family can also take the one-hour All Access Tour, which starts in the box office lobby under the distinctive Bulova Clock and continues through the arena, the theater's backstage, the luxurious Garden suites, the historic Walk of Fame, and the locker rooms of the Knicks and Rangers. Stand courtside on the Knicks floor, get behind the glass on the Rangers ice, and learn how the basketball court becomes a hockey rink. You never know whom you might see. Rock stars practicing for concerts, movie and TV stars in theatrical performances, and pro athletes have been known to pose for pictures. The tour is an exciting add-on if you're planning to attend a sporting event here, especially if your children are true sports fans.

GETTING THERE It's "easy" to drive here, but beware of traffic. By subway, take the 1, 2, or 3 (7th Avenue line) or the A, C, or E (8th Avenue line) to Penn Station or the B, D, F, N, Q, R, W, or PATH trains to 34th Street and 6th Avenue. The LIRR, NJ Transit, and Amtrak all stop in Penn Station. From Grand Central, take the S subway shuttle to Times Square and then a 7th Avenue subway. By bus, take the M4 or M10 here or any north–south bus to 34th Street and transfer to the M34 or M16 crosstown.

METROPOLITAN MUSEUM OF ART

At 2 million square feet, the Met, as it's known, is the largest art museum in the Western Hemisphere. Its permanent collection houses nearly 3 million works of art from all over the world, including objects from the Paleolithic era to modern times. If you spent a minute looking at each object here without taking a break, it would take more than 5½ years to see it all. So start small. Pick two to four areas to explore and plan to return. Free lectures and walking tours covering various parts of the museum and self-guided audio tours are available.

Certain areas of the Met are particularly fascinating to children, and yours will no doubt enjoy the Costume Institute on the ground floor as well as the musical instruments on the second floor by the American Wing's courtyard. Check out the collectors' baseball cards in the first-floor American Wing side gallery. And when it's time to take a break, relax on the benches in the courtyard of the American Wing, and admire the plantings and statues of a Native American and of a mountain lion and her family. In the Asian galleries, the Astor

KEEP IN MIND Strollers are permitted during all regular museum hours except Sundays, but you can borrow back carriers for free at the 81st Street entrance. Donations here also cover same-day admission to the Cloisters at Fort Tryon Park, if you're ambitious. The museum's gift shop stocks unusual kids' toys, games, and books, so it's a good source for birthday gifts that children won't already have. A wonderful addition to your home video collection is *Don't Eat the Pictures: Sesame Street at the Metropolitan Museum of Art*, starring Big Bird, Cookie Monster (at whom the title admonition is directed), and the rest of the gang.

Court Chinese garden showcases a Ming Dynasty scholar's courtyard, complete with water splashing over artfully placed stones.

Be sure to visit the popular Arms and Armor Hall, on the first floor, and the Egyptian Galleries. Check out the mummies and the Temple of Dendur, a real Egyptian temple moved here to save it from destruction. It's one of the most looked-at works of art in the museum. To make your visit into a treasure hunt, ask at the information desk for "Family Gallery Guides" and "Museum Hunts."

The museum's Web site contains fun facts and a list of daily family programs, most free with admission. Hello Met! is a great introduction, and a weekend family film series is popular. One-hour art workshops, such as Young at Art, are also offered. If you start slowly and with age-appropriate activities, your children can enjoy a lifetime of discovering this museum.

HEY, KIDS! Did you know that the colored buttons given to visitors show that they have made a donation (for admission) to the museum? More than 100 colors are used, and 17,000 buttons of the same color are given out each day.

EATS FOR KIDS There are many dining options within the museum. The **Cafeteria** and the **Café** are located near the 81st Street entrance. Take a stroll to the **European Sculpture Court Café,** or, from May through October, grab a light bite at **the Roof Garden Café,** both of which have nice views. Close by, grab a burger and fries at **Luke's Bar and Grill** (1396 3rd Ave., tel. 212/249–7070). Since 1925, the **Lexington Candy Shop** (1226 Lexington Ave., tel. 212/288–0057) has been serving milkshakes and malteds, cheeseburgers and crinkle fries to the luncheonette crowd. It's worth a trip back in time.

MUSEUM OF MODERN ART

Nicknamed MoMA, this museum maintains the world's foremost collection of 20th-century art: over 100,000 paintings, sculptures, drawings, prints, photographs, architectural models and drawings, and design objects. In summer 2002, this Manhattan icon is closing in preparation for the construction of a new building, and temporary exhibition space is opening in Long Island City, Queens. To celebrate the new MoMA QNS site, an installation of masterpieces from the MoMA collection will be mounted, including such pivotal artworks as Vincent van Gogh's *Starry Night* (1889), Pablo Picasso's *Les Demoiselles d'Avignon* (1907), and Andy Warhol's *Gold Marilyn Monroe* (1962). Have fun seeing how many of these masterworks you and your children can identify.

Aside from the art itself, MoMA will continue to offer its popular family programs at the Queens location. These include guided walks, gallery talks, art workshops, and film screenings, which introduce children and adults to the world of modern art. The Gallery Talks program, for children 4–10 and their parents, runs Saturday mornings before the

EATS FOR KIDS MoMA QNS's **Café** offers sumptuous sandwiches, soups, salads, and snacks on the mezzanine level. For a more formal, sit-down, family-style Italian feast, visit **Manducatis** (13-27 Jackson Ave., tel. 718/729–4602).

HEY, KIDS! The MoMA QNS site was once the Long Island City Swingline stapler factory. Check your desk drawers at home, and you'll probably find a Swingline stapler hidden there. The huge Swingline sign was clearly visible in the skyline as you approached New York City by car, train, or subway. Today the dramatic rooftop sign incorporates the MoMA logo and the added letters QNS (which stands for Queens), a play on the abbreviations used by airports—in New York as well as around the world.

museum opens to the public. Current programs include the One-at-a-Time drop-in program (children 5–10 and parents), in which families explore exhibits through lively discussion and gallery activities with a new theme each week. Tours for Tots, another Gallery Talk program (for 4-year-olds and their parents), introduces painting, sculpture, photography, and works on paper. The Gallery Talk's Two-in-a-Row series takes place on two consecutive Saturdays and is designed to help families sharpen their looking skills.

The Family Films program offers parents and children the opportunity to enjoy classic live action and animated short films followed by discussion with a museum educator and suggestions for follow-up activities in the museum. Family Art Workshops, geared to children 5–10 and their parents, let you explore artwork from the exhibitions followed by a hands-on art class. No matter what the age or level of art experience, participants in these varied family programs usually enjoy the experience of exploring art together.

KEEP IN MIND In spring 2002, museum operations move to the new MoMA QNS facility, and exhibitions there are scheduled for summer 2002 through late 2004. In late 2004 or early 2005, the new museum should open on 53rd Street. You can call the main number for up-to-date information on exhibits and construction, but you should call Family Programs (tel. 212/708–9805) to receive a current list of scheduled activities and detailed information on events for children.

MUSEUM OF TELEVISION AND RADIO

It's not hard to imagine what the attraction of this museum is, for students of radio and TV and families alike. The broadcast collection comprises over 100,000 TV and radio programs and advertisements from the 1920s to the present, and your family can enjoy radio and television programs at any of the museum's 96 consoles. Catch classic Jack Benny or early Ed Sullivan shows, watch the first moon walk, Uncle Milty, *I Love Lucy* reruns, or the Beatles' first appearance on American television. Other facilities here include four theaters and a radio-listening room, where you can drop in on curator-selected TV and radio shows. Pick up a daily schedule at the front desk.

Temporary exhibits, mounted regularly, have included a display of masks and costumes from *Star Trek,* with a peek behind the makeup of this very popular program, as well as Sesame Street's Art from the Fuzzy and the Famous, an exhibit of personal art from celebrity guests on the program, cast members, puppeteers, and special friends of the show, all compiled in celebration of the program's 30th anniversary. There's always something new in the

KEEP IN MIND If you'd like to watch vintage television footage or commercials, get to the museum early. Go to the library, and search a computer database for the program you want to view. Sign up for a time on an assigned console, and at the appointed hour your program "pops up" on your screen. Many consoles can accommodate more than one viewer, so you can watch with other family members. Another option is to enjoy the museum-selected screening series in some of the theaters.

temporary gallery spaces, with regular visitors returning frequently to check out the latest special screenings or exhibits.

On weekends from 11 to 2, children's programming from the museum's collection is shown, and on weekend afternoons in November, the International Children's Television Festival screens great children's television from around the world. Also included in this popular festival are interactive workshops with an international flavor, focusing on music, storytelling, and puppetry.

Frequently throughout the year, live radio broadcasts take place at the museum's on-site studio. Morning drive time, music, talk shows, and book chats are just some of the formats heard during these programs. These broadcasts are open to the public, and children will be able to see what happens behind the scenes of a radio show.

HEY, KIDS! If you're 8–13 and want to be on the radio, come for a Re-creating Radio workshop. No, you won't be the guest DJ on your favorite radio station—nothing that glamorous! Instead you can try re-creating performances and sound effects from shows of the '30s and '40s.

EATS FOR KIDS For a meal on a bun, visit **Burger Heaven** (20 E. 49th St., tel. 212/755–2166; 536 Madison Ave., tel. 212/753–4214). In the mood for tasty fries with taste-tempting toppings? Visit **B. Frites** (1657 Broadway, between 51st and 52nd Sts., tel. 212/767–0858). Also see Radio City Music Hall and Rockefeller Center and the Ice Rink.

MUSEUM OF THE CITY OF NEW YORK

Where in the world can you find seats from the original Yankee Stadium, a 1980 Checker cab, a piece of the old mechanical Times Square news "zipper," or a giant bolt tightener used to build the Brooklyn Bridge? At the Museum of the City of New York, of course! For more than 75 years this museum has gathered together the single most important collection of artifacts related to Gotham history. Today it houses over 1.5 million items, including more than 2,000 paintings depicting the changing cityscape and 500,000 photographs documenting city history.

Start by viewing the "Big Apple Video," shown every ½ hour. This 22-minute documentary tells the city's story through paintings, prints, photos, film clips, and other artifacts from the museum's extensive collections.

Since the four-story museum is too big to see in one visit, grab a floor plan, and take a vote on what to visit. Though the Period Room Alcoves, representing domestic life

EATS FOR KIDS Have a burger at **Peter's Burger Place** (1413 Madison Ave., tel. 212/722–4400). If you'd rather make your own salad or get soup or a sandwich, head for **Shin's** (1414 Madison Ave., tel. 212/831–1754), a deli-takeout joint with tables in a large room in back.

HEY, KIDS! Calling all children 7–10! You can join the museum's free MCNY Kids program and make history. On Saturdays from 11 to 12:30, member kids and an adult can create their own New York experience (no fee but preregistration advised). Tell a New York toy story. Paint the town. Make a portrait. Sing along with *Guys and Dolls*. Activities include guided gallery visits, art activities, walking tours, invitations to special events, quarterly newsletters, and a 15% discount at the Museum Shop. What are you waiting for? Be an MCNY kid!

1220 5th Ave., at 103rd St.

 Suggested donation
$7 adults, $4 students
6–college

 W–Sa 10–5, Su 12–5; T groups only

212/534–1672;
www.mcny.org

4 and up

from the late 17th to the early 20th centuries, may not be kids' favorite, the theater collection, including 3,500 costumes, might leave them starstruck. In the Fire Gallery, children learn about bucket brigades and see a hose carriage and pumpers that were pulled not by horses, but by firefighters. Youngsters are often fascinated with the toy collection in the New York Toy Stories gallery space, which features several hundred toys from Colonial times to the present, including antique dolls, children's games, and an unusual collection of furnished dollhouses from 1769 to the 1970s. Your kids can also visit the museum's collection of marine-related artifacts, including ship models, ships' figureheads, and paintings.

Like most good museums these days, this one is home to special exhibitions as well as walking tours, lectures, performances, readings, and family workshops open to the public. Unlike other museums, however, this one has as its subject the very city that it calls home.

KEEP IN MIND To get an in-depth look at the exhibits before you go, check out the Web site's Museum Collections Sampler, which includes pictures and information. In addition, some items and exhibits can only be seen on the Web, including New York Footnotes, a collection of 18th-century women's shoes from the costume collection. Also check out the 19th-century New York City valentine. Updated daily, the site contains a calendar of family events, too.

NATIONAL MUSEUM OF THE AMERICAN INDIAN

Adults find both the interior and exterior architecture of this museum as interesting as its collection of Native American artifacts. Children tend to be intrigued by the elaborate feathers, weavings and blankets, baskets, gold work, jade, Aztec mosaics, painted hides, Native American garments, and stone, wood, and horn carvings on display. But whatever your family's interests, you'll find plenty to see and do at this first museum of its kind dedicated to Native American culture.

In 1903, New Yorker George Gustav Heye began gathering a collection of 1 million Indian artifacts from North, Central, and South America. Eventually, it became New York's Museum of the American Indian, with Heye as director, but by late in the century it came under the Smithsonian umbrella, with the stipulation that it remain in New York. The National Museum of the American Indian also includes a research and conservation facility in Suitland, Maryland, and a museum currently being built on the National Mall in Washington, D.C.

KEEP IN MIND The museum offers programs of interest to the entire family that are fascinating, fun, and free. In May, a weekend afternoon Children's Festival has plays, storytelling, crafts, dance, films, museum talks, and hands-on learning activities. Screenings of documentaries and films by Native American filmmakers on contemporary subjects are shown daily, and storytelling sessions are also scheduled. Information regarding these and other activities can be found on the Web site.

George Gustav Heye Center,
1 Bowling Green

 Free

 F–W 10–5, Th 10–8

 212/514–3888;
www.si.edu/nmai

9 and up

The center occupies the first two floors of the Alexander Hamilton U.S. Custom House, a beautiful Beaux Arts–style building that is both a National Historic Landmark and a New York City Landmark. Outside are 44 columns, each adorned with the head of Mercury, the Roman god of commerce. Inside in the rotunda, a 140-ton skylit dome appears to soar overhead without any visible means of support. The symmetry of the Great Hall is complemented by monumental arches and columns.

The museum's collection spans more than 10,000 years of Native American heritage and includes cultural, historical, and artistic artifacts as well as items of spiritual significance. It's interesting to note that religious and cultural items are on display only with the approval of the appropriate tribes. Educational enrichment programs and presentations on living cultures are offered throughout the year. A resource center on the main floor contains a wide array of materials on Native American history and culture.

EATS FOR KIDS
Try tasty, tempting **Daily Soup** (55 Broad St., tel. 212/269–2336), a celebrity hangout with a great, modestly priced breakfast, brunch, and lunch. At **Bubby's** (120 Hudson St., tel. 212/219–0666), eat sandwiches, fish, or breakfast till late afternoon.

HEY, KIDS! Outside the building's huge entrance are four large sculptures, representing America, Asia, Europe, and Africa. The America statue features a Native American figure peering out from behind a throne. He wears a feather headdress and is surrounded by a totem pole and broken southwestern pottery. In 1907, when this customhouse was built, that Indian figure was meant to symbolize the vanishing Native American.

NBC STUDIOS BACKSTAGE TOUR

It's not a sure bet that you'll see any television stars, but you never know whom you may bump into on NBC's studio tour. But that shouldn't be the main reason to take this hour-plus behind-the-scenes tour. The real reason is to learn fascinating secrets of television production.

NBC has been offering tours since 1933. An NBC page serves as your guide through the peacock network, and who knows? Your page may go on to become famous, like former pages Ted Koppel, Willard Scott, Regis Philbin, Steve Allen, Kate Jackson, and Michael Eisner.

Tours begin and end in the NBC Experience, a museum and retail attraction directly across from *Today*'s Studio 1A, on the corner of 49th Street and Rockefeller Plaza. The museum features memorabilia from NBC's long history—the first Howdy Doody test pattern, a microphone from early radio, and a bottle from *I Dream of Jeannie*. Here you can also check out free interactive activities, such as a virtual interview with Jay Leno, Al Roker's Weather Challenge, or Conan O'Brien's Wild Desk Ride.

EATS FOR KIDS At the **Rock Center Café** (20 W. 50th St., tel. 212/332–7620), ask for a seat overlooking the skating rink in winter, the garden in spring–summer. Fans like **Mickey Mantle's** (42 Central Park S, tel. 212/688–7777) for its large portions, friendly service, oversize TV screens, and sports memorabilia.

HEY, KIDS! Want to attend a live taping of a TV show? *The Rosie O'Donnell Show* tapes Monday through Thursday here. Just ask a parent to write or call for information. You must be at least 5 to attend a taping—lower than the minimum ages of 6 for the tour and 16 to see *Saturday Night Live* live. Stand-by tickets are distributed at 7:30 the day of the show, outside on the 49th Street side of the building.

30 Rockefeller Plaza, 50th St. between 5th and 6th Aves.

 $17.50 ages 17 and up, $15 children 6–16

M–Sa 8:30–5:30, Su 9:30–4:30, tours every 15 or 30 min; longer hrs summer and holidays

212/664–3700, tapings 212/664–3056 or 212/664–3057; www.nbc.com/store

 6 and up

The tour itself starts in the NBC History Theatre, where Katie Couric and Matt Lauer of *Today* take you on a video journey through NBC's history. The walking tour includes a quick trip through two or three active studios—perhaps those of *Saturday Night Live, NBC Nightly News, Late Night with Conan O'Brien, Today,* NBC Sports, or *Dateline NBC*. You'll also learn about the latest TV technology, and production techniques are demonstrated in a mini-control room. Because of fast-breaking news and changes in broadcast schedules, the tour varies day to day. The final stop is the NBC/Panasonic HDTV Theater, where past and present NBC clips are used to unveil the future of High Definition Television.

Returning to the museum and retail site, you can play Bob Costas's sports trivia, purchase a souvenir picture of yourself on the virtual sets of your favorite shows, and direct your happy feet to the oversize floor chimes that play the NBC theme.

KEEP IN MIND Individual tickets can now be reserved and purchased in advance by phone or on-line with a credit card. You can also buy a combination ticket that includes a tour of Rockefeller Center (tel. 212/664–7174). Because so many groups book ahead of time, if you do choose to purchase your tickets on the day of your tour, you'll want to get here early. Tours are often sold out by early afternoon.

NEW VICTORY THEATER

Surprising as it sounds, this is Manhattan's first theater especially for families and kids. Its year-round season of professional productions by national and international artists is offered at surprisingly affordable prices. Reopened in 1995 as part of the theater district redevelopment, New York's oldest active theater was built in 1900 by Oscar Hammerstein. In 1902 impresario David Belasco took over the theater. Dramatic and vaudeville shows continued until 1932, when Billy Minsky opened Broadway's first burlesque in this theater. Next it was renamed the Victory, in the patriotic spirit of WWII, and ran second-run films for several decades. In the 1970s it became the block's first XXX-rated movie house. It seems emblematic of the whole Times Square face-lift that from these cultural ashes has risen a phoenix for families.

Along the way, it became "reel" famous, too, making appearances in such movies as *Manhattan Murder Mystery,* the original *Shaft, Taxi Driver,* and, most recently, *The Siege.* Renovation began in 1994, restoring the striking facade with its monumental second-floor entry

KEEP IN MIND The "New Vic" is wheelchair accessible, but wheelchair seats must be purchased in advance. In addition, some performances are sign-language interpreted. Booster seats for small children are also available. The benefits of membership include 30% discounts on tickets, priority seating (tickets available to members before they go on sale to the general public), a member-friendly exchange policy, newsletters, various contests, and coupons for local restaurants and other establishments. Members are also invited to free pre-performance workshops conducted by professional performers and guest artists, Each workshop highlights an activity related to the day's performance, such as juggling or dance.

staircase and globed standing lights. Inside, the opulent domed auditorium looks almost as it did as the Belasco Theater. Around the rim of the regal central dome are eight plump pairs of golden cherubs, whose feet dangle over the seats below. During the theater's renovation, the angels needed only one little repair—fixing a big toe. Adding to the elegant interior are tiers of box seats capped by golden domes. The two-balcony auditorium now holds 500 seats.

Cutting-edge family entertainment features masters of music, dance, drama, puppetry, and circus arts. Recent performances have included the Circus Oz, Arabian Nights, Parsons Dance Company, and Urban Tap. Performance times vary from just under an hour to two hours, and shows usually run two to six weeks. A new program for kids 13–18 lets them see a show in a teens-only section of the theater and gives them food, free stuff, and a chance to hang out with the show's cast. How cool is that?

EATS FOR KIDS
Try lunch, brunch, or dinner at **Zuni** (598 9th Ave., tel. 212/765–7626) for reasonable prices and southwestern flavors with Asian and Italian flair. You can't go wrong at **John's Pizza** (260 W. 44th St., tel. 212/391–7560). Also see restaurants in Broadway on a Budget.

HEY, KIDS! Now here's something to buzz about: If you count all the bees in the theater's wall moldings (added by David Belasco in 1902) and all the bees on the seat fabric (added by the New 42nd Street Inc. in 1995) plus all the ones on the metal chair sides at the end of each row, just how many bees are there in the New Victory? Final answer: There are 31,566 bees. Un-bee-lievable!

NEW YORK AQUARIUM

"**B**y the sea, by the sea, by the beautiful sea . . ." That little ditty conjures up images of crowded old seaside attractions like Coney Island. Alongside the cotton candy and amusements, however, is this aquarium, which first welcomed visitors in 1896 at its former site in Manhattan's Battery Park and moved to this 14-acre location in 1957. It's home to over 10,000 species of marine life, including beluga whales, giant sea turtles, sand-tiger sharks, and sea otters.

Don't miss the dolphin and sea lion demonstrations in the 1,600-seat Aquatheater, but don't sit too close either, unless you're prepared to get splashed. Get touchy-feely with a cow-nosed ray in the touch tank (May–October). Marvel at the re-creation of a rocky Pacific coast habitat for the aquarium's black-footed penguins; harbor, gray, and fur seals; sea otters; and Pacific walruses. Watch them from below water inside or from above water around rocks, trees, and pools outside. Check out the state-of-the-art wave machines, and try to attend one of the feedings throughout the day.

EATS FOR KIDS Eat a packed lunch on the Oceanic Deck or near Living Oceans, or buy from the outdoor **snack bar** or indoor **cafeteria.** Try boisterous, Italian **Gargiulo's** (2911 W. 15th St., tel. 718/266–4891) or **Totonno Pizzeria Napolitano** (1524 Neptune Ave., tel. 718/372–8606). The boardwalk has fast food.

HEY, KIDS! Take a "get wet" workshop, and prepare for oceans of fun. You can share the magic and mystery of the marine world through art, music, science, beach walks, lectures, tours, and other adventures. Free public events also are scheduled, ranging from an Amazon Adventure to the Halloween Sea Monsters program. Or dive right in and spend the summer as a Marine Explorer or Junior Oceanographer.

Boardwalk at W. 8th St., Coney Island, Brooklyn

 718/265-3400; www.NYAquarium.com

 $9.75 ages 13 and up, $6 children 2–12

 Memorial Day–Labor Day, M–F 10–5, Sa–Su 10–6; early Sept–late May, daily 10–5

 All ages

In Living Oceans, your family can stand under a 400-gallon tidal wave that crashes every 30 seconds. A Plexiglas hood keeps you dry, but the power of the sea may leave you breathless. Hands-on exhibits, interactive videos, games, and marine tanks teach about the ecology of the oceans and marshlands.

The Native Sea Life Exhibit houses an authentic shipwreck as well as the diverse aquatic life found in local waters. Come within inches of 9-foot sharks patrolling their 90,000-gallon tank. The Hudson River Exhibit relates the vital waterway's history and includes freshwater and marine habitats featuring sea turtles and moray eels. By the end of your visit, you might just be humming the rest of that ditty: "We'll have fun, we'll have fun, oh how happy we'll be!"

KEEP IN MIND A family membership in the Wildlife Conservation Society costs only $58 and lets everyone in your family visit the aquarium and the Bronx, Central Park, Prospect Park, and Queens zoos free for a year. Quite the bargain! You also get a year's subscription to *Wildlife Conservation Magazine,* a great read and valuable supply of school report pictures and articles for kids from kindergarten to college. (Trust me: You'll want to save these issues.)

NEW YORK BOTANICAL GARDEN

This 250-acre National Historic Landmark includes 48 gardens and plant collections including outstanding orchids, daylilies, flowering trees, and conifers; wetlands; ponds; a cascading waterfall; a 40-acre tract of the original forest that once covered the city; and dramatic rock outcroppings. But the reason families visit is the Everett Children's Adventure Garden, the first indoor/outdoor museum of botany and horticulture built especially for children. Its hands-on activities, imaginative exhibits, and fanciful gardens are exciting and inviting.

Stop at the visitor center for a free map and to check activity schedules. Then head for the Boulder Maze; explore its winding trail, and climb up to look through the discovery scope at the wetlands below. Next enter Beth's Maze, and find your way around the hedges. Sit or step on the oversize lily pads of the Sun, Dirt, and Water Gallery, and watch water shoot up. A giant frog topiary leaping from a splashing fountain invites you to discover how plants make food, move water, and use sunlight.

KEEP IN MIND The botanical garden is less crowded on weekdays, except Wednesday, when admission is free. A narrated tram tour, which runs every 30 minutes, lets you explore various places and spaces and reboard. Free guided walking tours on Wednesday, Thursday, Saturday, and Sunday as well as Monday holidays are probably best suited for older children. Weekend bird walks, at 12:30, are also free, as are audio tours of the conservatory's World of Plants, also available in a children's version.

In the Wonder Gallery, kids can invent a plant or wander through vine-covered tunnels, tiny bridges, and a minipond. At the outdoor Pond Gallery, kids can pretend to be a pond-dwelling animal. They can take a water sample and see what's in it, make a giant bird's nest, or visit the Plant Touch Tank. The Enid A. Haupt Conservatory, the nation's largest Victorian glasshouse, showcases rain forest plants, desert galleries, and numerous palm trees under glass.

The Children's Adventure Garden is part of the Children's Adventure Project, which also includes the Mitsubishi Wild Wetland Trail and the Ruth Rea Howell Family Garden. Along the wetland trail, children can get a close-up view of this fascinating ecosystem and discover What Stinks, an interactive exhibit about how wetlands recycle plants. In the family garden, visitors can dig; investigate ponds, insects, and plants; and meet gardeners from around the world. During the summer and winter holidays, annual trains add to the fun.

HEY, KIDS! Among the amazing plants here are the Venus's-flytraps. A bug a day keeps the plant doctor away. At 200 feet, the Kapok tree is one of the rain forest's tallest trees. Feeling hungry? Look for the cacao plant. Chocolate comes from seeds in its reddish brown pods.

EATS FOR KIDS The indoor/outdoor **Garden Cafe** serves kid-oriented comfort foods. Picnic tables are located at the Tulip Tree Terrace, near the Snuff Mill, on the Snuff Mill River Terrace, and outside the Children's Adventure Garden. Outside the garden in the Belmont section, also called Arthur Avenue, try one of the many pizza parlors and Italian restaurants. **Dominick's** (2335 Arthur Ave., tel. 718/733–2807) has inexpensive family-style Italian fare.

NEW YORK CITY FIRE MUSEUM

In a renovated three-story firehouse built in 1904, you and your family can view one of the most comprehensive collections of fire-related art and artifacts from the 18th century to the present. Large firehouse doors, the housewatch (front desk) entrance, stone floor, brass sliding pole, and hose tower remind visitors of the former home of Engine Company 30, its firefighters, its rigs, and its horses. The nonprofit museum operates in partnership with the New York City Fire Department, which owns the building and provides the collection and the firefighters who serve as tour guides.

Permanent and temporary exhibitions chronicle the evolution of fire-fighting technology beginning with the early bucket brigades. Carefully preserved hand-operated, horse-drawn, and motorized equipment; toys; models; fire engine lamps (running lights from horse-drawn equipment); presentation silver; oil paintings, prints, and photographs; "fire marks" (emblems on buildings denoting the brand of insurance carried); and folk art illuminate the traditions and lore of fire fighting.

EATS FOR KIDS Hankering for Cajun cooking and cowgirl memorabilia? Head to the **Cowgirl Hall of Fame** (519 Hudson St., tel. 212/633–1133). **Brothers Bar-B-Q** (225 Varick St., tel. 212/727–2775), a bi-level barnlike space, serves chicken and ribs; on Monday night, it's all-you-can-eat.

KEEP IN MIND Firefighter-led guided tours here are by advance reservation. During a tour, you can visit a mock apartment equipped with lasers, black lights, theatrical smoke, and other devices simulating and highlighting common fire hazards. The building can get crowded when group tours visit, so call ahead to see if schools are scheduled when you're planning to come. The museum also hosts birthday parties for children 4–8, and you can get fire-themed goodies from the museum store. To preview some of the museum's exhibits, read more about museum history, or get updates on family programs, visit the museum Web site.

278 Spring St.

212/691-1303;
www.nycfiremuseum.org

Suggested donation $4
adults, $2 students, $1
children 11 and under

T–Su 10–4

2–11

Organized fire fighting began in New York City in 1648, when eight fire wardens, nicknamed the Prowlers, patrolled the streets from dusk to dawn. These patrols were also called the Rattle Watch, as wooden rattles were the first fire alarms. Before phones were introduced in 1882, fire companies used the telegraph and a system of Morse code and bells to communicate fire emergencies across the city.

Preschoolers and early schoolers can learn why fires were a big problem in olden days and how bucket brigades worked. They may be fascinated by how men pulled and pumped the early fire engines and how horses and dogs helped. They may also discover how fire fighting changed as New York grew from a small village to a large city. Older students may be interested in the evolution of fire alarms, in the duties of today's firefighters, and in the teamwork involved in fighting fires. A Fire Safety exhibit especially for families features hands-on activities and information for whatever type of house or apartment you live in.

HEY, KIDS! Create your own scavenger hunt. On the first floor, look for those wooden rattles used as the first fire alarms. Since dogs have always been firehouse mascots, search for a dog collar. Can you locate an early motorized fire truck that was started with a hand crank? On the second floor, find the fire chief's sleigh and the engine with an eagle on top. This pumper rode in the parade for the newly unveiled Statue of Liberty over 100 years ago.

NEW YORK CITY OPERA YOUNG PEOPLE'S WORKSHOPS

No need to sing the praises of opera when you can experience it with your family at Lincoln Center. New York's amazing performing arts center is filled with theaters of all shapes and sizes, playing host to every type of music imaginable, dance, film, and even the circus. Of these, opera (the center is home to both the Metropolitan and New York City operas) is perhaps the least accessible for many children, but not to worry. The New York City Opera Young People's Workshops, offered by the New York City Opera education department, offer an energetic and exciting kid-oriented introduction to this musical and theatrical art form.

These one-hour interactive workshops are designed especially for families. Prior to select weekend matinee performances, City Opera staff and artists conduct hands-on activities that explore the themes, drama, and music of the afternoon's opera. Everyone is encouraged to join in the fun, which may include acting out a scene, learning a dance, examining costume design, or exploring a musical score. Four family-friendly operas are usually chosen each

KEEP IN MIND Like its bubbling, dancing fountain, Lincoln Center is over-flowing with wonderful family performances, from jazz to the circus, ballet to movies. Here's just a handful: the Chamber Music Society's Meet the Music Concerts for Kids (tel. 212/875–5788), Jazz at Lincoln Center (tel. 212/875–5599), Movies for Kids (tel. 212/875–5600), and the New York City Philharmonic's Young People's Concerts (tel. 212/875–5656 information, 212/721–6500 tickets). Though offered by the Metropolitan Opera Guild, the Growing Up with Opera program (tel. 212/769–7008) is usually held at a theater on the Upper East Side.

New York State Theater, Lincoln Center,
62nd St. and Columbus Ave.

 $5

 Sa-Su 12-1

212/870-5643; www.nycopera.com

6-12

season. Sessions have included such operas as *The Magic Flute, The Mikado, Porgy and Bess,* and *Carmen.* Advance reservations (which can be made on-line at the City Opera Web site) are required for the workshops, held at the New York State Theater between noon and 1. Doors, at the stage entrance, open at 11:30, and curtain is at 1:30.

If you need to brush up on your Verdi, Mozart, or Puccini, visit the New York City Opera Web site and access the Learning and Resource Centers. You can read biographies, explore an opera glossary, and locate plot descriptions so you can read the story before or after you hear the opera. And if you're wondering what to wear, pretty much anything goes these days. Some families do enjoy the occasion to dress up, but the key is comfort. Remember the aim is for everyone to have fun.

EATS FOR KIDS
To end your trip on a good note, try **Opera Espresso Restaurant** (1928 Broadway, tel. 212/799-3050), a glorified diner offering everything from chicken fingers to French cuisine. To see why New Yorkers like its brick-oven pizza, visit **John's Pizzeria** (48 W. 65th St., tel. 212/721-7001).

HEY, KIDS! If your interest has been piqued by the magic of opera, ask a parent if you can take a backstage tour of the Metropolitan Opera House (tel. 212/769-7020). Marvel at castle construction in the carpentry shop, suits of armor and Cinderella gowns in the costume shop, and big hair and bald pates at the wig-maker's shop. Peek into the rehearsal room, auditorium, dressing rooms, and cafeteria. Tours ($9 adults, $4 children 4-12), recommended for those 8 and up, are weekday afternoons and Saturday mornings. Reservations are advised for this 1½-hour tour, and potty stops are not included.

NEW YORK HALL OF SCIENCE

New York City's only hands-on science and technology museum is also one of the country's best. With more than 225 interactive exhibits over 35,000 indoor square feet (not to mention 30,000 outdoor square feet in the Science Playground), the hall is, scientifically speaking, *the* place to bring the family for a day of fun and learning.

The ground-level main hall contains Seeing the Light and Sound Sensations: The Inside Story of Audio, where kids jump and dance while their shadows "play" music. They can also compose a jazz melody and electronically change their voices. (Next stop: pop radio.)

The lower level contains the Hidden Kingdoms of the World of Microbes, with the largest collection of the world's smallest creatures. Also here are the Realm of the Atom and Marvelous Molecules—The Secret of Life. A new Biochem Lab is the world's first hands-on lab devoted to the chemistry of living things that's open to the public. Staff and step-by-step instructions help you conduct your own experiments.

HEY, KIDS!
Don't miss the Science Playground (April–November), the Western Hemisphere's largest outdoor laboratory of exciting whole-body experiences. Compose a tune with your feet on Sound Steps. Talk softly into the red Whisper Dish, and marvel when a friend across the playground can hear you.

KEEP IN MIND
Students with A's in both math and science can receive a free one-year Honors Membership to the museum, just another reason to hit the books. As for history, the hall of science is located in Flushing Meadow–Corona Park, site of the 1939 and 1964 world's fairs. Also in the park is the Queens Museum of Art (tel. 718/592–9700), in front of which is the Unisphere, easily spotted from miles around. First displayed at the 1964 World's Fair, this massive sculpture of the earth is 140 feet high and made from 380 tons of stainless steel.

47-01 111th St., Flushing Meadow Corona Park, Flushing, Queens

718/699-0005; www.nyhallsci.org

 $7.50 adults, $5 children 4–17; Th–F 2–5 free; Science Playground $2

 July–Aug, M 9:30–2, T–Su 9:30–5; Sept–June, M–W 9:30–2, Th–Su 9:30–5

 2 and up, Science Playground 6 and up

The upper level's Great Hall is home to traveling exhibits and a new permanent one: The Living Carpet. This large-scale interactive floor installation lets you explore and influence the emotional landscape of the carpet. What? You didn't think the floor had feelings? Don't miss the floor ballet of six interacting human silhouettes as it unfolds before your eyes. Also in this area is the kid-pleasing bubble area, where you and yours can create life-size bubbles or raise a bubble wall. Proceed with caution or you'll burst your bubble.

A 300-seat auditorium serves as a showcase for videos, films, lectures, and special events. Live science demonstrations are scheduled daily throughout the facility, and helpful staffers are stationed on all floors for demonstrations and assistance. In the Preschool Discovery Place, little hands can investigate sound, color and light, simple machines, and measurement apart from the bustling crowds that can be alarming to the under-6 crowd. For the over-6 crowd, the Science Access Center houses an extensive collection of books, videos, periodicals, CD-ROMs, and table-top activities.

EATS FOR KIDS No restaurants are really close by, so plan to pack a lunch and find a spot in the spacious 300-seat **dining hall** overlooking the park and Science Playground. No time to make a bag lunch? You can purchase sandwiches, snacks, and beverages from vending machines once you get here. The dining hall is available for children's birthday parties.

NEW-YORK HISTORICAL SOCIETY

Founded in 1804, the New-York Historical Society today serves as a collective memory of the heritage of New York City, the state, and our nation. Over 4 million items can be found here in vast collections of American paintings, sculpture, decorative arts, architectural materials, photographs, prints, books, and manuscripts. Where else could you go to learn about the 75-year history of the Macy's Thanksgiving Day Parade?

Step back in time to New York City in 1901 when you visit Kid City, a child-size re-creation of Broadway between 82nd and 83rd streets. You can learn the history of some of your favorite foods at the Amidon Market or stop in the Mehrtens' family bakery. You can also visit a typical turn-of-the-century family apartment to experience what life was like back then.

The Henry Luce III Center displays over 40,000 objects from the museum's collection. This dynamic laboratory and resource center allows visitors a behind-the-scenes look at a

KEEP IN MIND During the school break between Christmas and New Year's, the Historical Society celebrates the holiday season with special family programs each morning. Call the main phone number for a detailed schedule and registration information.

2 W. 77th St., at Central Park West

 212/873-3400;
www.nyhistory.org

 $5 ages 13 and up,
$3 students

 T–Su 10–5

5 and up

working museum collection. Here you'll find paintings, sculpture, tools, and furniture, including 132 lamps designed by Louis Comfort Tiffany.

Free family activities take place on Saturdays from 11 to noon for children ages 5–10 with an adult companion. Space is limited and pre-registration is strongly suggested. These popular interactive family programs may include crafts, dance workshops, storytelling, music, and puppetry.

Live performances in the arts, film festivals, walking tours, museum programs, and lectures round out the wide variety of public programs offered to families throughout the year.

EATS FOR KIDS
Cheap eats can be found at **Chirping Chicken** (350 Amsterdam Ave., tel 212/787–6631). Alternatively, make a reservation at **Ernie's** (2150 Broadway, tel. 212/496–1588), where casual dining, pizzas and pastas, kids' menus, crayons, and paper tablecloths perfect for doodling make this a sure bet to please the entire family.

HEY, KIDS! Be on the lookout for Inspector Collector, a.k.a. Harley Spiller, who has been known to host fabulous and fun family workshops on collecting. The inspector shows how collecting everyday items like spoons, postcards, and even chewing gum can teach us about American history and culture.

NEW YORK LIBERTY BASKETBALL

It's fast-paced, it's fun, it's family entertainment, and it's affordable. If this doesn't sound like today's professional sports to you, you haven't been to a New York Liberty game. The area's hot WNBA (Women's National Basketball Association) team plays summer basketball to Madison Square Garden crowds of just under 20,000, averaging second in overall attendance in the WNBA. They also happen to be the 1999 and 2000 Eastern Conference Champions, earning a spot in the finals in three of the league's first five years. It's not uncommon to spot celebrities like model Tyra Banks, actors Gregory Hines or Billy Baldwin, or rocker Joan Jett in the crowd.

Each season has 32 games, with half played at home at the Garden. Games usually run under two hours, unless overtime is called. Arrive early—gates open one hour before game time—to watch the pre-game shoot-around and team warm-up. Technically, no photographs are permitted, but young fans with cameras do snap shots of their favorite players before the games. Souvenir team yearbooks are $3.

HEY, KIDS! Hey basketball fans and surfers, log on to the Liberty's Web site to catch up with your favorite team. You can e-mail questions to the team's head athletic trainer or directly to the team. Other features take you behind the scenes to learn all about the team and the game they play. You can also click to find out about special promotions and give-away nights. And if that's not enough, New York Liberty runs a girls' summer basketball camp (tel. 212/924–4040 ext. 106) each year. It's a slam dunk!

During the games, look for Maddie the Mascot, a friendly overgrown dog, making friends with the fans, leading the conga lines on the court, and leading the cheers. Also part of the excitement here is the 12-member Torch Patrol. This athletic, high-energy squad of young men and women conduct fun, frenzied mayhem during time-outs, incorporating tumbling, dance, and crowd interaction. At each game, the arena's most spirited section of fans is chosen to attend a post-game autograph session with team players, so get your wave ready and make your cheer loud and clear. And don't even think about leaving your seat during halftime, or you'll miss the entertainment. When was the last time you got to see Frisbee-catching dogs or bike stunts? Don't try this at home. But do practice your hook shot and keep dribbling.

EATS FOR KIDS
The **Houlihan's** (2 Pennsylvania Plaza, tel. 212/630–0349) chain of restaurants is known for its kid-friendly fare, balloons, crayons, and appealing adult menu. Another chain known for its family cuisine is **T.G.I. Friday's** (484 8th Ave., tel. 212/630–0307). Go for the burgers, sandwiches, or salads.

KEEP IN MIND Promotions take place during nearly every game. Whether it's miniball or sports-poster giveaways, mascot day or fan appreciation T-shirt night, these special events give your kids another thrill just by walking through the turnstile. The team also holds celebrations like Flag Day, Father's Day, and charitable game promotions like a Cheering for Children Auction and Breast Cancer Awareness Night. Check the Web site for updates, and if you have a choice, pick a game where they're giving something away.

NEW YORK TRANSIT MUSEUM

When is a museum not an ordinary museum? When it's housed in a decommissioned 1936 subway station in downtown Brooklyn. The New York Transit Museum is a walk-up, sit-down, and touch museum that is home to 100 years of transit history and memorabilia. The collections include 19 restored subway cars dating from 1904 to 1964, as well as antique turnstiles, a working signal tower, a surface transportation room, and a variety of other transit equipment.

Revolving exhibits, programs, workshops, and tours provide an insider's look at MTA bridges, tunnels, subways, buses, and commuter railroads. You and your children can watch a film clip about the age of Els (elevated trains) before they fade into history. Take the A Train or catch all the trains you missed in an exhibit of full-size classic wooden cars and their modern counterparts. Or see a sign of the times in a display of nearly 200 examples of subway signage: in porcelain enamel, cast iron, brass, wood, and plastic. Pass through the first automated turnstiles. Drive a city bus, or better yet, don't miss the museum's

EATS FOR KIDS The **Armando Ristorante** (143 Montague St., tel. 718/624–7167) offers traditional Italian fare at more than fair prices. For other food choices, see the Brooklyn Academy of Music and Brooklyn Botanic Garden.

KEEP IN MIND The museum offers guided tours of different parts of the transit system in Manhattan, the Bronx, Queens, Brooklyn, Staten Island, and Long Island, and some include excursions to historical and cultural destinations. Because some tours involve strenuous walking and stair climbing, wear sturdy and comfortable shoes and clothes. Bring your MetroCard or tokens for travel, but first call ahead for reservation information and fees.

Boerum Pl. and Schermerhorn St.,
Brooklyn Heights

718/243-8601;
www.mta.nyc.ny.us/museum

$3 adults, $1.50
children 3–17; some
workshops charge

T–F 10–4, Sa–Su 12–5

2 and up

annual Bus Festival, in late spring or early summer. An entire block is shut to park historic buses outside, including a wooden open-top double-decker bus and a favorite, the 1949 Jackie Gleason bus, modeled after the one driven by Ralph Kramden on *The Honeymooners*.

Shopping for a (subway) token of your affection to give to a (nostalgic) loved one? Look no further than the Transit Museum Gallery and Store. For transit-related toys, trinkets, and memorabilia, this is the place. In addition to the shop inside the museum, there's another one at Grand Central Station, adjacent to the Station Masters' Office, and a Transit Museum Store and Travel Information Center at the Times Square Visitors Center (east side of Broadway, between 46th and 47th Sts.). Admission to the Museum Gallery at Grand Central and to the New York Transit Museum at the Times Square Visitors Center is free.

HEY, KIDS! Each year the museum conducts some nifty workshops just for kids. You can build a working model of a suspension bridge, make your own bus model, or create poetry in motion by writing your own poster poem like the ones on subways and buses. Or sign up for a special workshop with New York City Transit engineer Vinny Voltage (Vollano). His science sessions include chemistry, physics, electricity, and mechanics in an awesome and magical demonstration not to be missed.

NEW YORK UNEARTHED

There's history underfoot when you step inside New York Unearthed, the South Street Seaport Museum's off-site urban archaeology museum. Here the remains of the past tell the story of New York's colorful history. In fact, the program focuses on interpreting the lives of centuries of New Yorkers through the objects they left behind: Native American arrowheads, Dutch clay pipes and delft tiles, fragments of Chinese-export dinnerware, a silversmith's tools, children's marbles, and even animal bones, which reveal in detail the dietary habits of early residents.

Don't miss the Unearthing New York Systems Elevator, which whisks your family down through the layers of a simulated dig beneath the city streets. Your children can explore a three-dimensional cross-section of an archaeological site and view archaeologists and conservators at work in a fully equipped conservation laboratory. The professional staff is always happy to answer questions as they process some of the museum's 2-million-artifact collection. They could be piecing together fragments of dinnerware or puzzling over the origins of a

HEY, KIDS! Time travel is possible when you spend a week at the South Street Seaport Museum's Dig It! Archaeology Camp. You can discover the amazing secrets buried beneath the skyscrapers of New York in five-day sessions, offered during July and August for kids 8–11. Campers piece together artifacts, make crafts, meet special guests, play 19th-century games, and take a lunch cruise along the East River on archaeological adventures. Space is limited to 15 per session.

17 State St., at Battery Park, in courtyard on Pearl between Whitehall and State Sts.

 Free; some programs charge

 M–F 12–6

 212/748–8628; www.southstseaport.org

 4 and up

piece of weathered wood. Did it come from a ship? A building? Was the wood grown locally or was it brought from across the sea? Answers to these questions can help fill in the missing pieces of the past that are not found in written history lessons.

The archaeological collections of eight nearby scientifically excavated urban sites include approximately 7,000 exhibit-quality artifacts, which help illuminate the worlds of merchants, artisans, slave traders, slaves, seamen and their families, grocers, boardinghouse keepers, and the children who lived in lower Manhattan from the days of New Amsterdam to the early 20th century. Public programs include demonstrations, lectures, performances, workshops, walking tours, and guided museum tours, which focus on the themes of tenement life, early tools, 17th- to 19th-century diet, artisans' workshops, and trade. In a city bursting with unusual experiences, this one is truly unique, and as hard as it is to believe, admission is free. Can you dig it?

KEEP IN MIND New York Unearthed has expanded programming to provide educational experiences for all ages—from preschoolers to seniors. Founded on the belief that people learn in many ways, the exhibits and activities here are not only age appropriate but also appeal to different learning styles through visual, tactile, and auditory stimulation. Grandparents and great-grandparents can perhaps relate what they see to what they lived or heard about, so why not bring them along to enrich everyone's experience?

NY WATERWAY FERRIES

18

I n the early 1800s, New Yorkers traveled to and from Manhattan by ferry, but as bridges and tunnels were constructed, ferries fell out of favor. Today, you can experience this form of transportation on NY Waterway, the largest private ferry operation in the nation. NY Waterway transports over 7 million passengers into the city each year on 22 vessels covering eight ferry routes. For commuters, ferries offer a shortcut to Manhattan minus the traffic jams, tunnel and bridge tolls, and parking problems usually associated with car travel. Ferry crossings run anywhere from five to eight minutes, with frequent departures throughout the day.

Ferries aren't just for commuters, however. If your family wants to sightsee, you can take a fun-filled ride and glide to ports of call in and around New York—to the beach at Sandy Hook, New Jersey; around lower Manhattan; and up the Hudson River, just to name a few. Most terminals offer all-day parking, and a free private shuttle bus system operates throughout the city, providing service to tourists, commuters, and downtown residents.

HEY, KIDS!

If you're taking a ferry to a Yankee game, why not make it a doubleheader of sorts? Ask your parents to find out about tours of Yankee Stadium (tel. 718/579–4531). Highlights include the dugout, press box, clubhouse, and Monument Park.

KEEP IN MIND The best sightseeing bargain in the city is the free 20- to 30-minute ride on the Staten Island Ferry (tel. 718/390–5253) across New York Harbor. Take the older model blue and orange ferries, which sail higher in the water and have outside deck space, so you can enjoy views of the Manhattan skyline, the Statue of Liberty, Ellis Island, the New Jersey shore, and the Verrazano Narrows Bridge. Ferries run every 15 minutes during rush hours, every 20–30 minutes most other times of the day and evening, and every hour after 11 PM and on weekend mornings.

Terminals in Manhattan and New Jersey

 800/533-3779; www.nywaterway.com

 Fares vary depending on destinations, packages, and tours; 50% discount children 3–12

 Schedules vary, depending on route

 2 and up

Sightseeing tours around lower Manhattan include harbor cruises by day and twilight cruises providing up-close views of the Statue of Liberty, Ellis Island, and the Brooklyn Bridge. You can also take a ferry to see the Mets or Yankees play ball. Packages include ferry transportation, a ticket to the game, a hot dog and beverage, and a souvenir. Dining and Broadway show packages are also available.

Hudson River cruises include tours of the legendary Rockefeller family estate in Pocantico Hills and historic Philipsburg Manor, a working Dutch Colonial farm; a Sleepy Hollow Cruise, including Sunnyside, the home of Washington Irving, and Philipsburg Manor; a scenic trip down the North Hudson River without stops; and a cruise to Lyndhurst, a great Gothic revival–style estate. But as nice as these sights are, what's really special about the tours is seeing New York from the water.

EATS FOR KIDS Some boats have a **snack bar** selling snacks, soft drinks, and cocktails. On some sightseeing cruises, box lunches are served, and passengers often take them ashore and eat at the historic sight being visited. Dining packages include reservations at various city restaurants. If you're taking NY Waterway from Weehawken, New Jersey's Port Imperial Terminal, consider eating right at the marina at **Arthur's Landing** (Pershing Rd., Weehawken, NJ, tel. 201/867–0777), which has a kids' menu.

PLAYSPACE

If it's raining, it's pouring, and it's getting boring, pack up your rambunctious youngsters, and head to PlaySpace, the city's first walk-in indoor playground just for kids 6 and under. Here they can jump, run, dig, play, sing, slide, eat, crawl, skip, splash, tumble, hop, laugh, and talk to their hearts' content (and yours).

PlaySpace contains all sorts of areas that appeal to youngsters with all sorts of interests. There's plenty of room for an Olympic-size sandbox; a two-story firehouse; a train; a toddler labyrinth; a 6-foot twisting slide; bridges, tunnels, and other climbing structures; a child-size stage; dress-up costumes; and more. A changing program of concert events takes place Monday through Thursday.

PlaySpace is not just a place for parents to sit and kids to run around. There's plenty of opportunity for parent and child interaction, creativity, and fun—all in a clean, safe, and

KEEP IN MIND Naturally, Manhattan has other indoor playgrounds (check the Yellow Pages). For gymnastic classes (6 months–12 years), contact **Jodi's Gym** (244 E. 84th St., tel. 212/772–7633) to arrange a free trial class. For older children, try sports and recreation centers: **Hackers, Hitters & Hoops** (123 W. 18th St., tel. 212/929–7482) features batting cages, Ping-Pong, basketball, an obstacle course, video games, and miniature golf. **LaZerPark** (1560 Broadway, tel. 212/398–3060) has LaZer Tag and video, arcade, and token games. **ExtraVertical Climbing Center** (61 W. 62nd St., tel. 212/586–5382) is an indoor climbing gym for beginners to experienced climbers.

2473 Broadway, at 92nd St.

 $7.50 players

 Daily 10–5:30

 212/769–2300;
www.playspaceny.com

 6 mth–6 yr

challenging free-play environment. Huge age-specific play areas, storytelling, arts and crafts, child-size hoops, and tons of toys round out the experience. From simple to sublime, PlaySpace also offers two-hour birthday party packages in two private party rooms.

The staff is warm and welcoming, and the rest rooms—containing changing stations and a kid-size bathroom—are clean. Safety flooring protects against injury from falls and tumbles, and for summer comfort, the complex is air-conditioned. You'll probably also be happy to know that all equipment and toys are disinfected nightly and the sandbox is raked daily, sifted once a week, and changed every month. Now if only they'd had a place like this when you were a kid!

HEY, KIDS! In addition to plain-old play, PlaySpace offers varied classes. Topics include music, ballet, and baby games. (You can even tell Mom and Dad that they offer parenting workshops.) So find out what's coming up. You might want to stop, look, and learn before (or after) you leap.

EATS FOR KIDS PlaySpace has a healthy **snack bar** on the premises for parents and kids. The **Popover Cafe** (551 Amsterdam Ave., tel. 212/595–8555) is very child-friendly, dotted with teddy bears in various nooks and crannies. Comfortable booths and hearty food welcome family diners. The original location of **Carmine's** (2450 Broadway, tel. 212/362–2200) serves heaping family-style servings of Northern Italy's best comfort food. Come hungry.

PROSPECT PARK

Prospect Park offers 526 acres of winding paths, rolling hills, open spaces, and great green places to stroll, picnic, fly a kite, feed the ducks, or sit and think. Modeled after Central Park, it is home to the 75-acre Long Meadow, one of the city's greatest open spaces, with spectacular views of grass, trees, and sky. Feed the ducks and spot the swans at 60-acre Prospect Lake (Brooklyn's only freshwater lake), or stroll through the Oriental Pavilion.

If you want to ice-skate, head for the Kate Wollman Center and Rink from mid-November to early March, near the Lincoln Road entrance. It's the only open-air rink in the borough. Skate rental is available, and instruction is offered by the New York Skating Center. Most of the rest of the year, this is the place to rent pedal boats, which seat four—a great way to take a break and a tour of the lake at the same time.

A 1912 carousel, in operation from April to October but not every day, features 51 magnificently carved wooden horses, along with a lion, giraffe, deer, and dragon-drawn

KEEP IN MIND Prospect Park hosts special community events throughout the year, including a Girl Scout Camporee, ethnic parades, and festivals. Free Celebrate Brooklyn Concerts are held at the Bandshell (Prospect Park West and 9th St.), mid-June–Labor Day. Music ranges from jazz to bluegrass, classical to zydeco.

HEY, KIDS! For a haunting good time, join the Halloween Haunted Walk and Festival held at Prospect Park the last Saturday in October from noon until 3; it's near the Nethermead (the geographical center of the park). You'll be in ghoulish company as thousands of visitors walk along the haunted park pathways. Watch out for witches, ghosts, goblins, and other creatures that go bump in the night—or, in this case, the afternoon. Don't miss the kiddie carnival with games and prizes.

Eastern Pkwy. and Grand Army Plaza, Brooklyn

718/965-8899 park, 718/789-2822 children's museum; www.prospect-park.org

Free; some attractions charge

Daily sunrise-1 AM; children's museum W-F 1-4, Sa-Su 1-5

9 mth and up

chariots. This magnificent piece of Americana, originally installed at Coney Island, is located at the Willink entrance at the intersection of Empire Boulevard and Flatbush Avenue. For live animals, head to the Prospect Park Zoo (see #15).

Last but certainly not least is the Lefferts Homestead Children's Museum, in one of the few surviving Dutch Colonial farmhouses in Brooklyn. Today it plays home to kids who play house in this historic building. It is the only historic house in the city that is home to a children's museum. Though there are two period rooms furnished with antiques, your children can play in four rooms furnished with reproduction furniture, interactive toys, and games. A dollhouse replica of the Lefferts Homestead provides another way to play with the past. Seasonal programs, storytelling, theater, and music are ongoing throughout the year, and family volunteer programs offer opportunities for families to work, play, and learn together.

EATS FOR KIDS A short walk from the Bandshell, the **Living Room Cafe** (199 Prospect Park West, tel. 718/389-0824) is located in the historic Pavilion Theater, once a single-screen movie house but now a multiplex. Have a sandwich, a sundae, an egg cream, or crepes as you watch the strollers in the park. **Kate's Corner Snack Bar** (Kate Wollman Center and Rink) is open Thursday through Sunday.

PROSPECT PARK ZOO

This 12-acre zoo, completely revamped and transformed into a modern children's wildlife learning lab, is home to 82 species of animals. Naturalistic habitat exhibits have replaced bars, cages, and pits, and the larger species that were part of the original menagerie of the late 1800s and early 1900s are gone.

Enter the Animal Lifestyles building, and your children will find air, water, and land animals in exhibits related to the center's wildlife education program. Reptiles, amphibians, fish, birds, and small mammals help highlight the environments they live in and their adaptations to their homes. The centerpiece of the building is the 4,500-square-foot hamadryas baboon exhibit. Perched high on the rock cliffs by an impressive waterfall, separated from these fascinating social primates by an invisible sheet of glass, their somewhat less fascinating primate cousins (humans) feel very much a part of this exhibit. Don't be surprised if a friendly baboon approaches the glass to study you back.

EATS FOR KIDS A **cafeteria** is near the sea lion pool. Visit the **Second Street Café** (189 7th Ave., tel. 718/369–6928) for lunch or brunch. Order soup and some raisin-studded bread pudding. Try **Two Boots** (514 2nd St., tel. 718/499–3253) for creative pizzas (including Cajun), pasta jambalaya (for adventurous kids), paper tablecloths, coloring books, crayons, and a restroom changing table. (Can you guess why it's called Two Boots?) Other neighborhood kid fare is listed under the Brooklyn Botanic Garden.

450 Flatbush Ave.,
Prospect Park, Brooklyn

 718/399-7339;
www.wcs.org

 $2.50 ages 13 and
up, 50¢ children 3–12;
programs extra

 Apr–Oct, M–F 10–5, Sa–Su 10–5:30;
Nov–Mar, daily 10–4:30

All ages

Drawing supplies are provided in the Animals in Our Lives building. Playful meerkats, emerald tree boas, saw-whet owls, and poison dart frogs call this space home. In a second area, staffers discuss pet care and what species should *not* be domesticated. In a barnyard, kids can peek into the chicken coop or meet goats, sheep, and cows. California sea lions frolic in a rocky California coast–like environment.

Innovative prekindergarten programs have inviting themes like Bedtime at the Barn, Baboon Breakfast, and Animal Crackers. Other kids' programs are available on a first-come, first-served basis through mail-in registration. Some run over school vacations or overnight and have included a Spooky Sleepover, Zoo Dreams, and a Polar Pack-In. The zoo also sponsors special community events—the Fleece Festival, Keeping up with Keepers, Boo at the Zoo, and Make a Wish for Wildlife—free with admission. All in all, it makes for wonderful family fun.

GETTING THERE You'll find entrances off Flatbush Avenue and near the Lefferts Homestead. If you drive, you can find free parking on Flatbush Avenue. By public transportation, take the subway's S or Q train to the Prospect Park station or the B41, B47, or B48 bus.

HEY, KIDS! Want to really experience animal habitats? Visit the World of Animals' 2½-acre Discovery Trail. Burrow in Plexiglas-topped tunnels, and pop up next to a prairie dog. Leap-frog across lily pads to goose nests, and pretend to hatch. In the Wallaby Walkabout, you can walk among these small Australian kangaroos and other animals, and in the 2,500-foot aviary at trail's end, you can walk around free-flying African birds and climb into nests your size. Willoughby Wallaby Whew!

PUPPETWORKS

For more than 35 years, the Puppetworks, Inc., under the artistic direction of Nicolas Coppola, has been known throughout the country for its mostly marionette productions. In 1987 Puppetworks opened a permanent 75-seat theater in a Park Slope (Brooklyn) storefront, conveniently located next to the Puppetworks workshop. Puppet performances are also staged part-time at the Children's Aid Society's Greenwich Village Center Theater. These informal and family-friendly theaters present daily performances of children's literature classics, with weekdays reserved for groups (20 or more). Puppetworks also hosts private showings of their programs for on-site birthday parties. You supply the cake; they supply the entertainment and the clean-up.

Favorites like *Puss in Boots, Rumpelstiltskin,* and *Pinocchio* may round out a year-round season that might also include the *Wizard of Oz,* a gala *Carnival of the Animals, The Frog Prince, Peter and the Wolf,* and *Alice in Wonderland.*

EATS FOR KIDS In the Village, try coal-fired pizza at **Arturo's** (106 W. Houston St., tel. 212/677–3820). In Park Slope, go to **Two Boots** (*see* Prospect Park Zoo) or, for crispy pizza, **Lento's** (833 Union St., tel. 718/399–8782).

KEEP IN MIND Since 1976, when Macy's built a gingerbread puppet theater for Puppetworks, more than 50,000 children and their families have attended the annual Puppetworks Christmas performances. Bring your family to Macy's Herald Square (Broadway at 34th St., tel. 212/695–4400), and start a new tradition. The holiday-themed performances are given 10 times daily and cost only a few dollars. Macy's recently built a new puppet theater for these always festive and well-attended family puppet programs.

338 6th Ave., at 4th St., Brooklyn; 219 Sullivan St., between W. 3rd and Bleecker Sts.

 Brooklyn $7 adults, $6 children 17 and under; Manhattan $8 adults, $6 children

 Brooklyn Sa–Su 12:30 and 2:30, Manhattan some Su 1:30 and 3:30

718/965-3391; www.puppetworks.org

 2–12

Just two puppeteers are responsible for each performance, and while each show averages 13 puppet characters, some have had up to 68 puppets. The professionally designed sets and intricate puppet costumes give the feeling of a "slightly scaled-down" Broadway show. At the end of many performances, one of the professional puppeteers will bring out a puppet to show to the audience, giving a brief behind-the-scenes—or, more accurately, above-the-strings—talk about the workings of a puppet theater.

In the spirit of artistic cooperation, other puppeteering troupes from across the country often appear here, too.

HEY, KIDS! The walls of the Brooklyn Puppetworks theater display close to 100 marionettes used in past performances, though many are re-used and recostumed. Can you identify the characters or the stories they come from? If you can't, let your imagination wander. Try to think of fairy tales you know. Who's the scariest villain, the cutest animal, your favorite character? Do any of the puppets you see look like them, and how do they differ from the way you would have created them?

QUEENS COUNTY FARM MUSEUM

A farm in New York City? Just barely. At the very edge of Queens, the Queens County Farm Museum occupies New York City's largest remaining tract of natural, undisturbed farmland. The landmark farmhouse and the 7-acre farmyard that make up the museum are just a small piece of the 47-acre Adriance Farm Park.

The farm was started in 1772 and passed through a series of owners until 1927, when New York State purchased the farm for Creedmoor Psychiatric Hospital, to provide both fresh produce and therapy for its patients. Staff and patients raised crops and livestock until the program was discontinued in 1960. Through the Colonial Farmhouse Restoration Society of Bellerose, organized in 1975, the farm's historic structures were preserved and the site was turned into a city park.

Pick up a map and take a self-guiding tour of the farm museum. Begin at the centerpiece of the restored farm: the colonial farmhouse, where much of the original 18th-century plank

KEEP IN MIND Of the many family programs here, most carry a fee and some require reservations. (A calendar of events is listed on the farm Web site.) Activities have included a fall Apple Festival, Barnyard Easter Egg Hunt, arts and crafts workshops in winter and spring, New York's Annual Antique Auto Show, a weekend Civil War encampment, the Queens County Fair, and the Thunderbird American Indian Mid-Summer Pow Wow. A summer program of arts, crafts, and nature courses for children 6–10, comprising three two-week sessions, is offered, as are one-hour summer arts and crafts workshops for children 4–5.

73-50 Little Neck Pkwy., Floral Park

 Free; some events charge

Sa–Su 12–5, plus Th 12–5 May–Sept; outdoor farm areas M–F 9–5

718/347–FARM;
www.queensfarm.org

1 and up

floors, beamed ceilings, wainscoting, paneling, doors, window glass, and hardware has survived. Other areas available for touring include the duck pond, the herb garden, and the orchard. A chicken coop houses 100 free-range hens producing 260–290 large brown eggs each laying cycle. The eggs are collected daily and washed and boxed for sale. Your children can visit Daisy, an Ayreshire cow, in the cow shed and stroll by the sheep pastures to survey the grazing livestock. Fields are planted with corn, pumpkins, tomatoes, and other vegetables.

Each season the farm wears a new face, whether it's welcoming newborn barn animals in spring or picking the fresh produce of summer, stomping through the snow paths in winter or crunching a crispy autumn apple. The Queens County Farm Museum offers a thick slice of farm life to you and your family, painting a picture of the city's rich agricultural past.

HEY, KIDS! Contribute to the Fund-A-Friend program, and you'll get a certificate and your name will be included on a display at the farm. Funds raised are used for feed and veterinary care, from $8 for a chicken or duck to $100 annually for a "caretaker," helping all the animals.

EATS FOR KIDS You can't beat the price or the selection at the lunch buffet at **Pizza Hut** (253-11 Hillside Ave., Bellerose, tel. 718/343–1118). Thanks to kids' meals, you can feed a child for under $4 and yourself for under $7. Hop on over to **IHOP** (248-16 Northern Blvd., Little Neck, tel. 718/224–1178), short for the International House of Pancakes, to indulge in breakfast all day long. It's a sure-fire bet for pancake lovers, especially kids who love different flavored syrups.

QUEENS ZOO

Once upon a time, Flushing Meadow played host to the 1964 World's Fair. A zoo opened on the fairgrounds in 1968, and in 1992 it was completely revamped, transforming itself into this small but friendly 11-acre zoo, home to 400 animals of some 40 species. Here you can come face to face with a mountain lion, see South American spectacled bears at play, and watch Roosevelt elk roaming the range.

You can walk on the wild side from one coast of the United States to the other. Visit re-created habitats from a northeastern forest to the Great Plains to the rocky California coast. Stroll from the forest floor to the treetops of the zoo's walk-through aviary (a geodesic dome designed by Buckminster Fuller for the World's Fair) to view a variety of birds. Cross the covered viewing bridge of the coyote exhibit to peek into a window on their world.

The marsh exhibit forms a habitat for ducks, geese, herons, egrets, and turtles. The bison range lets you watch these fascinating American symbols from various points, giving the effect of the Great Plains of long ago. A waterfall, additional trees, and rock formations have improved the habitat for the endangered South American spectacled bears. Don't forget to say hi to Claire, the bald eagle named for Queens Borough President Claire Shulman.

On the domestic side of the zoo, youngsters can meet and touch goats, sheep, and rabbits in an inviting planted space where they can also see a llama, Vietnamese pot-bellied pig, zebu, Jersey steer, donkeys, and such feathered friends as a Peking duck and Rhode Island red. Despite its size, the zoo offers something for just about everyone.

KEEP IN MIND The zoo is located next to the New York Hall of Science, both in Flushing Meadow Corona Park. Combine your visit to either place with a stop at the nearby Queens Museum of Art (New York City Building, tel. 718/592–9700) to see the 9,335-square-foot scale model of New York City—complete with 895,000 tiny buildings and landmarks—originally made for the 1964 World's Fair.

RADIO CITY MUSIC HALL

You may have watched an awards show broadcast from Radio City Music Hall or even attended a performance here, but to get behind the scenes of this lavish Art Deco palace that's home to the high-kicking, smart-stepping Rockettes, you'll want to take the Grand Tour. The brainchild of theatrical impresario S. L. "Roxy" Rothafel, owner of New York's Roxy Theater, Radio City was the first building in the Rockefeller Center complex and the world's largest indoor theater in 1932. In 1999, it was renovated at a cost of $70 million. Tours showcase the building's technological capabilities as well as its history. Luminaries such as Frank Sinatra, Ella Fitzgerald, and Sammy Davis, Jr., have graced this stage, as have contemporary artists including Bette Midler, Sting, and 98 Degrees.

To whet your appetite, here are some amazing Radio City facts: Some of the curtains can create steam and rain, and the shimmering gold curtain is the largest theatrical curtain on earth. The mighty Wurlitzer organ, built in 1932, has two consoles, each weighing 2½ tons. Its pipes, some of which are 32 feet tall, are housed in 11 rooms. Look up and you'll

KEEP IN MIND In 1979, to save the music hall from the wrecking ball, the program format was changed from films and stage shows to live concerts, television specials, and events. The *Radio City Christmas Spectacular, Sesame Street Live,* and adult as well as kid concerts play to sell-out crowds throughout the year. We're guessing you probably won't get an invitation to a big awards show, so you'll have to pay to attend one of these performances if you want to see a show at this extraordinary venue. It's worth the price.

260 6th Ave., at 50th St.

212/247-4777;
www.radiocity.com

Tour $16 ages 12
and up, $10 children
11 and under

Tours daily 10–5 every ½ hr

7 and up

see a 24-carat gold-leaf ceiling glistening 60 feet above you. For the electrical record, the music hall contains over 25,000 light bulbs inside; outside, the marquee is a block long and has more than 6 miles of red and blue neon.

The tour also includes a visit to the private apartment of founder Roxy Rothafel and a stop in the costume shop, which contains examples of lustrous outfits worn by the Rockettes, the world's most famous precision dance troupe. Your tour group will also meet a member of the Rockettes, who will share some of the company's history. One-hour tours depart every ½ hour from the main lobby at the corner of 6th Avenue and 50th Street.

And once your family has taken the tour, consider joining the over 300 million people who have seen movies, concerts, special events, and stage shows here over the years, and see all that technological wizardry at work yourselves.

HEY, KIDS! Imagine all the people and events that have graced this famous stage: from Madonna to Barney, the MTV Video Music Awards to the Tonys. The movies *Snow White and the Seven Dwarfs, 101 Dalmatians, Miracle on 34th Street, The Lion King,* and *GoldenEye* all premiered here.

EATS FOR KIDS Take your pick (or your children's pick) of local theme restaurants, each with eye-appealing memorabilia and kid fare. Music fans sing the praises of the **Hard Rock Cafe** (221 W. 57th St., tel. 212/459–9320). Movie buffs marvel at **Planet Hollywood** (1540 Broadway, tel. 212/333–7827). Board a space-ship to planet Mars for a crater burger, galactic cheese sandwich, or full moon pizza at **Mars 2112** (1633 Broadway, tel. 212/582–2112).

ROCKEFELLER CENTER AND THE ICE RINK

It's enchanting, its twinkling, it's festive and fun, and when the huge Christmas tree presides over the Ice Rink at Rockefeller Plaza, it's spectacular. It may not be the biggest rink in the world, but skating here certainly is one of the big New York experiences. Skate and locker rentals, season passes and multiticket books, lessons, and group rates are all available, as are birthday parties (January–April). Teens get a bit exuberant during evening skates and the pace is faster, but day or night, it's a skate to remember.

But the ice rink is just a small part of the 22-acre complex known as Rockefeller Center, one of the world's most famous pieces of real estate. There are actually 19 limestone and aluminum buildings here, and tours of the complex as well as combination tickets including a tour of NBC studios (see #29) are available. Or explore the center on your own, before or after your skating session.

EATS FOR KIDS Dine by the rink at the **Rock Center Cafe** (see NBC Studios Backstage Tour), or try the **Harley-Davidson Cafe** (see American Folk Art Museum). **Dean & DeLuca** (1 Rockefeller Plaza, tel. 212/664–1363) serves quick sandwiches and snacks. See also the Museum of Television and Radio and Radio City Music Hall.

KEEP IN MIND Other great spots for a twirl on the ice are the Lasker and Wollman Memorial rinks (see Central Park), the latter offering a magical experience beneath the city skyline; Sky Rink (see Chelsea Piers); the World's Fair Ice Skating Rink (New York City Building south wing, Flushing Meadow Corona Park, Queens, tel. 718/271–1996); the Staten Island Skating Pavilion (30-80 Arthur Kill Rd., Staten Island, tel. 718/948–4800); and Brooklyn's Kate Wollman Center and Rink (see Prospect Park), not to be confused with Central Park's similarly named facility. Contact each for prices, hours, and seasons.

Travel this complex moving east to west, following a trail punctuated by three famous statues from Greek mythology. Atlas stands guard outside the International Building (5th Ave. between 50th and 51st Sts.). Head one block south on 5th Avenue and turn west to stroll along the Channel Gardens, which lead from 5th Avenue to a stair connected to the Lower Plaza. Six rock pools are surrounded by flower beds filled with seasonal plantings in a setting conceived by artists, floral designers, and sculptors who present 10 shows each year. Somehow it manages to look great in any season. Below on the Lower Plaza, locate the famous gold-leaf statue of Prometheus, towering heroically over the ledge. The entrance of the 70-story GE Building (30 Rockefeller Plaza), once known as the RCA Building but now referred to as "30 Rock," is also guarded by another striking statue of Prometheus, recently regilded and refurbished. It all makes Rockefeller Center a landmark of epic proportions.

HEY, KIDS! The GE Building houses NBC headquarters (*see* NBC Studios Backstage Tour), and some of the first television programs originated from here. Nowadays *Today* broadcasts from a ground-floor glass-enclosed studio at 49th Street and Rockefeller Plaza. Be here between 7 and 9 AM to try to join the backdrop of faces behind the show's hosts. Bring a colorful sign saying hello to a loved one or proclaiming your hometown (if you're from out of town). You might get on TV.

RYE PLAYLAND

Go for the rides. Go for the fun. Go to sun, swim, play, or walk around, but go to Rye Playland.

This National Historic Landmark, opened in 1928 and featured in such films as *Big, Fatal Attraction,* and *Sweet and Lowdown,* still counts seven of its original rides among its more than 45 rides. But the park also features a new vertical thrill ride, water rides, and a separate Kiddyland just for the toddler set. (You'll even find pony rides here.) The carousel, built in 1915, is still going strong, and the trademark 82-foot Dragon Coaster is one of the last remaining historic wooden coasters in North America. Don't miss the spinning Inverter, Dream Machine, and Mind Scrambler—well, perhaps parents would just as soon miss these sensory experiences. Also at the park are arcade games, the usual midway games, a lake with boat rides, minigolf, a beach, a boardwalk to amble on, and an Olympic-size pool, all on Long Island Sound.

KEEP IN MIND Remember to bring all the essentials: swimsuits, towels, beach toys, sunscreen, and water bottles—especially for your younger thrill seekers. Unlike the rest of this beautifully landscaped park, Kiddyland has no natural shade (or cool breezes). Bring blankets or lawn or beach chairs if you're staying for a concert. And of course, bring money. Parking costs $5 weekdays, $7 weekends, and to ride the rides you can purchase individual tickets or ticket books ($8.50–$20), providing a reduced rate. Look for $2–$3 discount coupons in local magazines and newspapers, and if you find one, don't leave it at home.

Playland Pkwy., Rye Beach

Free; most attractions charge

May–Sept, T–Su, hrs vary seasonally

914/813–7000;
www.ryeplayland.org

All ages

To plan your day, start at the beach or pool, before the sun gets too hot, and lunch and munch on the boardwalk. By afternoon, it's off to the rides, along with a round of minigolf and a boat ride. Rides usually open at noon, and Tuesday through Friday (the park is closed Mondays, except for summer holidays and special events) are less crowded than weekends. Be warned that Kiddyland gets crowded by midday, so you'll want to visit early or at dinner time. By early evening you'll be ready for a concert, usually staged on Thursdays in late July and August. Parents and kids can bop to songs of the '70s, '80s, and '90s. Fireworks displays are held every Wednesday and Friday night in July and August.

Maintained by the Westchester County Parks Department, this old-fashioned amusement park is a beautiful setting dotted with Art Deco buildings straight out of the 1920s, meticulously groomed flower beds, and grassy, shady malls for strolling. It's a delight!

GETTING THERE The park is less than a 45-minute drive from the city. Take I-95 (the New England Thruway), and get off at Exit 19. Follow the signs to Playland Parkway. Or call Westchester County Bee-line Buses (tel. 914/682–2020) for schedules.

EATS FOR KIDS It's hard to imagine coming here without letting your children sip slushies or get sticky with cotton candy for a snack break. There are sit-down tables and fast food galore throughout Playland, including favorites from fast-food giants **Burger King, Nathan's Famous,** and **Ranch 1.** You can also pack a lunch and use the picnic tables. The foot-long kosher hot dogs, ice cream, candy apples, and fried dough are hard to resist. Cruise the boardwalk for additional fast-food fare.

SCHOMBURG CENTER

8

The Schomburg Center for Research in Black Culture, one of the research libraries of the New York Public Library system, is considered one of the leading institutions of its kind in the world. Devoted to the preservation of materials on black life, it is the guardian of over 5 million items, including over 3.5 million manuscript items, 170,000 books, and 750,000 photographs. Collections of magazines, posters, art objects, films, videotapes, audio recordings, and memorabilia are also included.

Tours, exhibitions, forums, film screenings, and performing arts bring black history and culture to life for both young and old. Thanks to a 350-seat state-of-the-art auditorium, a 75-seat theater/auditorium, and a 30-seat screening room, the Schomburg Center sponsors over 60 programs each year, including poetry readings, plays, concerts, lectures, and panel discussions. Regular exhibitions are mounted in the gallery and exhibition hall. The Art and Artifacts collection holds over 20,000 items in three areas: paintings and sculpture, works on paper, and textiles and artifacts. It is particularly strong in art produced

EATS FOR KIDS Go to **Manna's Too!! Deli Restaurant** (486 Lenox Ave., tel. 212/234–4488) for breakfast, salad bar, fried chicken, and soul food buffets. For southern specialties, home-style cooking, and friendly service, try **Miss Maude's** (547 Lenox Ave., tel. 212/690–3100) or **Sylvia's** (328 Lenox Ave., tel. 212/996–0660).

HEY, KIDS! Inlaid in the floor of the airy lobby of the Langston Hughes Auditorium is *Rivers*, an artistic work that's a tribute to Hughes (1902–1967), writer of plays, stories, books, newspaper sketches, and, most notably, poems. If you haven't read anything by him, read his poem "A Dream Deferred." He penned many of his Jesse B. Semple or "Simple" columns about Harlem life in a brownstone at 20 East 127th Street, between Madison and 5th avenues.

Free
 515 Malcolm X Blvd.

212/491-2200;
www.schomburgcenter.org

M–Sa 10–6, Su 1–5

 9 and up

during the Harlem Renaissance. Portraits of many famous 19th- and 20th-century black artists, politicians, actors, musicians, athletes, and social activists are included.

Take time to look at Africana Age: African and African Diasporan Transformations in the 20th Century, an exhibit that details the political and cultural achievements and struggles of the black world during the last century. It also looks at the challenges facing peoples of African descent in this new century. Whether in sports, literature, politics, religion, music, entertainment, art, or other fields, people of African descent have made tremendous contributions to society despite unbelievable odds. See how many of these achievers you and your children recognize. Discuss the contributions each one has made to society. If your knowledge is lacking, there is no better place to learn about the influence of black Americans on our history and culture than the Schomburg Center.

KEEP IN MIND Other Harlem sights include the Abyssinian Baptist Church (132 Odell Clark Pl. W, tel. 212/862–7474), pulpit for two famous Adam Clayton Powells, one of whom was also a congressman. Tour the Apollo Theatre (253 W. 125th St., tel. 212/749–5838). The Studio Museum in Harlem (144 W. 125th St., tel. 212/864–4500), a small art museum, has a sculpture garden and a collection of paintings and photographs. Off the beaten path but worthwhile is the American Numismatic Society (Broadway at 155th St., tel. 212/234–3130) and its coins and medals.

SONY WONDER TECHNOLOGY LAB

7

From the moment you are greeted outside the Sony Wonder Technology Lab by b.b. wonderbot, the interactive telepresence robot, you feel the excitement of cutting-edge communication technology. Enter your name, have your picture taken, and record your voice at the log-in station, located at the twinkling fiber-optic lights, to obtain your personalized "swipe cards," which allow access to four floors of exciting and inviting interactive exhibits.

For a historical perspective, the Communications Bridge covers 150 years in the history and development of technology. Look for red circles along the way, which highlight important inventions. And just think: One day, all these exciting new technologies will just be red circles in some future historical display.

Don't be surprised if you see your picture or hear your voice pop up throughout your visit. You're not just going to see technology; you will become part of it during an adventure of

KEEP IN MIND This place is a true bargain. Admission to this nifty wonderland of technology is free, as are screenings of popular movies shown evenings in the theater. Even the children's workshops, scheduled on select Saturdays and Sundays, cost only a moderate fee. Students in grades 1–12 can take part in innovative and creative sessions in which they can learn the science of animation, create their own video short, produce a family video documentary, or dissect the similarities between the human eye and the camera.

550 Madison Ave.

Free

 T–W and F–Sa 10–6, Th 10–8, Su 12–6

212/833–8100;
www.sonywondertechlab.com

All ages

hands-on educational fun. Don't despair if you and your kids are not techno-whizzes; helpful guides throughout the lab will answer your questions and offer assistance.

Okay. Roll 'em, as your children take part in a production in the television studio or join the crew to edit a music video by a Sony artist. They can visit the Environmental Command Center, where they'll need to gather and analyze data using the latest tools and technology in order to save the day.

Finally, take a break in the 72-seat High Definition Theater, where you can sample the latest in High Definition Television, coming soon to a TV near you.

EATS FOR KIDS
In Sony Plaza, a **kiosk** has bagels, sandwiches, and soups for a picnic in Central Park, and **Starbucks** (tel. 212/833–6102) offers sandwiches, cookies, and desserts. **Mangia** (16 E. 48th St., tel. 212/754–7600; 50 W. 57th St., tel. 212/582–5882) has tempting sandwiches, salads, and antipasto.

HEY, KIDS! He's a mess of wires, microchips, and a whole lot of attitude. He's b.b. wonderbot, the lab's robot star and official greeter. Wonder how he can answer all the questions he's asked? Telepresence technology! What's that? Go behind the scenes to learn about this technology and learn the secrets to his remarkably lifelike movements and his conversational style.

SOUTH STREET SEAPORT MUSEUM

Nestled within a 12-block historic district of restored 18th- and 19th-century buildings and sailing ships, this museum actually comprises a number of facilities: a visitor center, Children's Center, Maritime Crafts Center, library, three galleries, a fleet of sailing ships, and re-created printing shop as well as the off-site New York Unearthed (see #19). All are dedicated to chronicling the history of New York's original seaport and its commercial and cultural impact on the city, the state, and the nation.

Set sail for another place and time with a map and schedule from the visitor center. Whether it's a sea chantey serenade, guided tours, or family programs, there is always something happening at the museum. Family Gallery Guides direct you around temporary exhibits on the port's history. Over 2 million archaeological artifacts, fine and decorative folk arts, ship models, scrimshaw, and maps are showcased in the Whitman, Melville, and Port Life galleries.

HEY, KIDS!

If a visit here tickled your sails, come back for the weekend Maritime Madness program (ages 8–12). Learn to furl a sail, tie a knot, or chart a course, and earn a sailor's certificate. Other weekend programs, for the whole family, focus on history, science, and the arts.

EATS FOR KIDS

Grab a burger, hot dog, pizza, or salad at the **Promenade Food Court** (Pier 17, 3rd floor). Don't miss the view from the tables in the glass-walled atrium. For hearty, sumptuous soup try **Seaport Soup Company** (76 Fulton St., tel. 212/693–1371). You can also get it to go. For casual breakfast, lunch, dinner, or Sunday brunch, **City Bakery** (3 W. 18th St., tel. 212/366–1414) can't be beat. Try the pretzel croissants or the inventive salad bar, or sample homemade ice cream at the soda fountain.

Visitor center, 12 Fulton St.; Children's Center, 165 John St.; Whitman, Melville, and Port Life galleries, Water St.

 212/748-8600; www.southstreetseaport.com

 $5 ages 13 and up

 Apr–Sept, Th 10–8, F–W 10–6; Oct–Mar, W–M 10–5

 3 and up

Three historic museum vessels are open for tours, including the *Peking* and the *Wavertree* (large sailing cargo ships) and a lightship, the *Ambrose*. Explore the harbor on the *W.O. Decker,* a 1930 tugboat that worked this waterfront. Or climb aboard the *Pioneer,* a historic schooner, for a fun-filled ride. Sailing instruction for teens is offered on the *Lettie G. Howard,* a fully restored 1893 fishing schooner, now a National Historic Landmark.

Your family can visit the Maritime Crafts Center, where model-builders and a wood-carver ply their trades. At Bowne & Company, Stationers, a re-creation of a 19th-century printing shop, artisans demonstrate the skills that made the city the nation's printing capital. The museum's Children's Center offers interactive exhibits, family programs, and educational games that make history come alive for children. On weekends, holidays, and school vacations, crafts workshops related to museum themes and exhibits are held. Performers and storytellers are also featured periodically.

KEEP IN MIND Also in the district, see the Titanic Memorial (Fulton and Water Sts.), a small lighthouse commemorating the 1912 sinking. Follow Fulton Street's cobblestones to Schermerhorn Row, a redbrick terrace of Georgian and Federal warehouses and countinghouses housing shops and restaurants. Go for a museum tour the first and third Wednesday of the month, April through September. Or, until the Fulton Fish Market moves to the Bronx in 2003, take a 6 AM guided tour through the nation's largest and oldest (since the 1820s) wholesale fish market.

STATEN ISLAND CHILDREN'S MUSEUM

How would your children like to crawl through an ant home, watch a butterfly being born, or listen to an insect chorus? They can do that and more at the Staten Island Children's Museum. Located in an 82-acre park, the museum occupies 10,000 square feet of a four-story building boasting an Italianate facade. An imposing porpoise, hanging in the central atrium, greets you. Exhibits tackle subjects from many different perspectives, incorporating the arts, science, and the humanities with an inviting child-friendly approach.

The Bugs and Other Insects exhibit invites big and not-so-big people into the miniature world of insects. If insects bug your kids, a quick trip to Block Harbor will put them back on an even keel. This waterfront setting, complete with pirate ship and gangplank, is an imaginative play space containing blocks and a menagerie of animal toys. Kids jump right in to the Wonder Water exhibit, which highlights the unique properties of that vital part of our world. A collection of tubs and sinks, boats, water wheels, terrariums and aquariums, and a babbling brook beckon.

KEEP IN MIND You can become family members of both the Staten Island Zoo and Staten Island Children's Museum for $80. Membership benefits include admission to both, as well as admission to more than 100 reciprocating zoos in the United States and Canada; advance notice of special events; sneak previews for new exhibits; invitations to "members only" events; discounts on gift shop purchases, museum birthday parties, special programs, and summer minicamps; special offers from local businesses; the zoo magazine and calendar; and the museum newsletter.

Snug Harbor Cultural Center, 1000 Richmond Terr., Staten Island

 $4 ages 2 and up

 July–Aug, T–Su 11–5; Sept–June, T–Su 12–5

 718/273–2060; www.sichildrensmuseum.org

 2 and up

Meet you in the Animal Diner, part of the Animals Eat: Different Feasts for Different Beasts exhibit. Here children can find out what the live animals are having for dinner and learn about the food chain. Portia's Playhouse is an interactive theater space where kids try on masks or costumes and use props, puppets, sound effects, lights, and other theater equipment in imaginative play. The Walk-In! Workshop is a classroom activity center equipped with self-directed art activities and materials. The Big Adventure is a wacky game where kids can climb a wall of rocks, crawl through dark tunnels, and tackle other physical challenges.

Founded in 1974 by a group of parents, the museum moved to its current site in 1986. Interpreters are always on hand to animate and explain exhibit themes and activities. School and community programs, traveling exhibits, family workshops, hands-on science activities, and performances of storytelling, dance, drama, and puppetry are all part of the fun and learning here.

EATS FOR KIDS
Goodfella's Brick Oven Pizza (1718 Hylan Blvd., tel. 718/987–2422) will make you an offer you can't refuse: great pizza. Try the killer chili at **Adobe Blues Restaurant** (63 Lafayette St., tel. 718/720–2583), a south-western-style eating place just off Richmond Terrace.

HEY, KIDS! There are so many different ways to "do" this museum. Want to watch the stars come out here? The museum sponsors sleep overs. Feel like celebrating? You can have a birthday party here, perhaps based on a museum exhibit, or a cooking, a chocolate, or an ice cream party, too. During school holiday recesses, the museum offers many exciting programs, free with admission, whereas "make and take" craft sessions carry a materials fee.

STATEN ISLAND ZOO

How many legs does an African millipede have? How far can a snowy owl turn its head? How big is a baby King Island wallaby when it's born? For the answers to these and other animal queries, visit the Staten Island Zoo. On 8 acres in a manicured park setting, New York City's biggest little zoo features an African savanna, aquarium, and tropical forest.

The African Savannah exhibit re-creates this ecosystem at twilight and features meerkats, a burrowing python, leopards, bush babies, and rock hyrax—curious creatures that look like rodents but are actually most closely related to elephants. The Tropical Forest exhibit highlights the endangered South American rain forest and the animals that dwell within. Here your family can watch the piranha, spider monkeys, ocelots, short-tailed leaf-nosed fruit bats, and iguanas in a natural flow of flora and fauna.

The wraparound aquarium exhibit spotlights marine life from all over the world, whereas the Children's Center resembles a New England farm, complete with a covered bridge

HEY, KIDS!

Snakes Alive! If you love things that slink and slither, check out the Carl Kaufeld Serpentarium, which features an internationally acclaimed display of reptiles. In fact, it has one of the most extensive collections of North American rattlesnakes anywhere.

KEEP IN MIND Plan your day at the zoo so you don't miss the action during feeding times. The reptiles chow down at 2:30 PM on Sunday. The sharks and piranha at the aquarium break for a bite at 1 on Thursday. (Don't worry. They do eat more than once a week; they just don't eat in front of an audience at other times.) Join the bats from 2 to 3 every day for a meal in the Tropical Forest.

614 Broadway, Staten Island

 718/442-3100;
www.statenislandzoo.org

 $3 ages 12 and up,
$2 children 3–11,
W 2–4:45 free

 Daily 10–4:45

 All ages

overlooking a duck pond. Here your children can meet an interesting array of international domestic farm animals. Be sure to visit the Pony Barn and Track.

Special programs are held throughout the year with some—like Breakfast with the Beasts, Kids and Critters, and Sleepy Time Stories—requiring preregistration and a nominal fee. Other events—like Reptile Realities, Setting Up a Home Aquarium, and Make It and Take It—are free.

The zoo is a great place to celebrate Groundhog Day. Chuck, New York City's only weather-predicting groundhog, greets visitors throughout the day after a 7:30 AM prediction proclamation. Hardy souls who brave the cold to cheer the resident rodent share coffee, juice, bagels, and the fun of witnessing Chuck's moment in the sun (or shadow).

EATS FOR KIDS Visit the **snack bar** (tel. 718/720–7218) for a convenient lunch or midday snack. Or try the neighborhood **Kings Arm Restaurant** (500 Forest Ave., tel. 718/448–0326) for family dining and a wide selection of tantalizing menu items. For homemade ice cream and old-fashioned soda-fountain treats, go to **Egger's Ice Cream** (1194 Forest Ave., tel. 718/981–2110).

STATUE OF LIBERTY

"**G**ive me your tired, your poor, / Your huddled masses yearning to breathe free. . . ." Many people recognize the opening lines of the poem "The New Colossus," which is inscribed on a plaque inside the Statue of Liberty museum. Everyone recognizes the sentiment. For over 100 years, this historic monument has served as a universal beacon of hope and opportunity, a symbol of freedom, and a gift of international friendship. It is one of our nation's most heavily visited attractions, popular with both kids and adults. The official name of the statue is *Liberty Enlightening the World,* and for over a century, she has done as her inscription reads: "I lift my lamp beside the golden door."

The statue was sculpted by Frederic-Auguste Bartholdi, who first traveled to America in 1871 to propose the monument and choose a suitable site. Built in 1884 in France, the statue stood in Paris until it was dismantled and sent to the United States in 1885. A foundation and pedestal were created here, and the completed monument was dedicated on October 28, 1886. By the 1980s, a complete refurbishment was needed, and a team of

KEEP IN MIND Security measures may affect your visit to this American treasure. For the latest information, don't rely on the Web site—be sure to call. In summer, crown access is limited to passengers on the first and second ferry boats and it's not uncommon to wait 2–4 hours to climb. There's no shade, and waiting can be hard on kids; bring water bottles, juice boxes, and small toys to amuse them. Saturdays are more crowded than Sundays. It's a good idea to ask how long the wait for the crown is before buying tickets. The ticket office for both the Statue of Liberty and Ellis Island ferry service is at Castle Clinton National Monument (*see #57*), a restored brick fortress in Manhattan's Battery Park.

French and American artisans worked for two years repairing and replacing as necessary to keep the sculptor's original creation shining in the harbor. In 1986, the fruits of their labor were harvested, as the statue celebrated her centennial.

One of the main reasons to visit the statue, of course, is to view this monument to freedom up close. Many older children will want to try to climb to the crown of Miss Liberty. Most don't get to the top. But even those who venture no further than the pedestal will have much to see and do. A museum here features exhibits detailing how the statue was built, and the promenade, colonnade, and top level of the pedestal offer spectacular views of New York Harbor. Videos of the view from the crown are shown for those unable to make the climb to the top, and life-size castings of the face and foot of the statue are available for sight-impaired visitors to feel. As she always has, Lady Liberty welcomes all.

EATS FOR KIDS
There's a pleasant outdoor **café** on Liberty Island. You can also pack a picnic to eat along the way, or after your return on the ferry, go to one of the eateries mentioned in Ellis Island, Fraunces Tavern Museum, New York Unearthed, and South Street Seaport Museum.

HEY, KIDS! Ready for the climb to the crown? If you're really ready for a challenge, you can climb the whole thing—364 steps (the equivalent of 22 stories) from bottom to top. You're not allowed to go up into the torch, though. Sorry! Or if mom and dad *insist*, you can take an elevator 10 stories to the top of the pedestal, where there's an awesome view of Manhattan.

THEODORE ROOSEVELT BIRTHPLACE

Though the building here isn't the real brownstone where Teddy Roosevelt was born—it's a 1923 reconstruction—it does teach a lot about the real life of the nation's 26th president. Five period rooms—the library, dining room, parlor (the most elegant room in the house), master bedroom, and nursery—are furnished with many items from the original house, pieces belonging to other family members, and other decorative period pieces. Two obelisks in the library are souvenirs of a family trip to Egypt. The horsehair chair seats in the dining room are said to have scratched Roosevelt's legs during his early childhood. In addition, two museum galleries display a variety of historical items, including journals, family photographs, political buttons and cartoons, articles of clothing including Roosevelt's Rough Rider uniform, and his crib.

The site offers a window on what mid-19th-century life was like for a wealthy family living on a once-quiet, tree-lined street in a most fashionable New York City neighborhood. Memorabilia reveals much about the man who would become not only president of the

KEEP IN MIND For those interested in following TR through his later years, visit the Sagamore Hill National Historic Site (Cove Neck Rd., Oyster Bay, tel. 516/922–4788), on Long Island. Roosevelt's home for most of his adult life, it contains original furnishings and memorabilia.

HEY, KIDS! Do you have a favorite teddy bear? The teddy bear was actually named for Teddy Roosevelt, who once refused to shoot a captive bear on a hunting trip. Political cartoonists poked fun at the incident, but a Brooklyn toy maker asked Roosevelt's permission to make stuffed bears and call them "Teddy's bears." The upper museum room has one of these original bears along with cartoons, books, writing paper, ceramic figures, and other objects with teddy bear images. Does your bear look like one of "Teddy's bears"?

28 E. 20th St.

 212/260–1616

 $2 ages 17 and up

 W–Su 9–5

7 and up

United States but also vice president, governor of New York, assistant secretary of the Navy, police commissioner, New York State assemblyman, and Rough Rider, as well as a rancher and cowboy.

As a young child, Theodore, called Teedie by his family, was a thin and sickly child who suffered from severe asthma. His father made the bedroom behind his nursery into an open-air porch by taking out a wall and putting up a railing. He also installed gym equipment so Teedie could exercise and improve his health. Roosevelt and friends used to climb through the nursery windows to get to the outdoor porch and equipment. He obviously overcame his frailty.

The Life and Times of Theodore Roosevelt, a 30-minute documentary narrated by Walter Cronkite, highlights Roosevelt's life, including scenes of 19th-century New York City. *Teedie,* also a 30-minute film, tells the story of the young Teddy who lived here. Other biographical films are sometimes shown as well, and concerts, lectures, and special events are scheduled throughout the year.

EATS FOR KIDS For a spot of tea and a light snack, visit **T Salon & Emporium** (11 E. 20th St., tel. 212/358–0506). For an endless menu, substantial portions, and reasonable prices, try **America** (9 E. 18th St., tel. 212/505–2110). On weekends kids get crayons and coloring books, and a magician and balloon artist perform on Sunday.

UNITED NATIONS

If you come on a working day, you'll see all 189 U.N. members' flags flying above 1st Avenue—from Afghanistan to Zimbabwe. It's an impressive sight, but so are the rest of U.N. Headquarters and the United Nations itself. Created in 1945, it joins countries working for world peace and against poverty and injustice.

As you enter headquarters gates, you're stepping into an "international zone," belonging not just to the United States but to all member nations. It has its own fire and security forces and its own postal administration, where you can post only mail bearing U.N. stamps. Mail a postcard to yourself as a souvenir.

One-hour guided tours include an explanation of the aims, structure, and activities of the organization as well as descriptions of art and architecture featured en route. Tours are given in many languages. What else would you expect at an institution with six official languages: Arabic, Chinese, English, French, Russian, and Spanish?

1st Ave. and 46th St.

 Tour $7.50 adults, $4.50 students grades 9 and up, $3.50 students grades 1–8

 Daily 9:15–4:45; tour daily every ½ hr, except Jan–Feb, no Sa–Su tour

212/963–7713, 212/963–7539 non-English tours; www.un.org

 8 and up, tour 5 and up

On most days, tours take in many of these areas: General Assembly, Security Council Chamber, Trustee Council Chamber, Economic and Social Council Chamber, Rose Garden, lobby, and public concourse. In the lobby, noteworthy gifts to the U.N. include a model of Sputnik I from the Soviet Union, moon rock from the United States, a statue of Poseidon from Greece, and a 15-foot by 30-foot stained-glass Chagall window presented by the artist in memory of Secretary General Dag Hammarskjold. Other artworks include the mosaic *Dove of Peace,* presented by Pope John Paul II, in the General Assembly lobby; *Non-violence,* a bronze replica of a revolver tied in a knot, from Luxembourg, outside by the General Assembly building; and a Norman Rockwell mosaic, near the Economic and Social Council Chamber, inscribed, "Do unto others as you would have them do unto you." In truth, your children might practice the golden rule better than some U.N. members, but amazingly, after over 50 years, this organization still strives to unite very disparate nations.

KEEP IN MIND Surfing isn't just for kids. At the U.N. home page, you can take an on-line tour before your visit; get up-to-date information about U.N. work in areas like peace and security, economic and social development, and human rights; and browse press releases and daily highlights, often before printed versions are released. You can also get free publications (in several languages) from the U.N. and many of its agencies and programs.

extra! extra!

CLASSIC GAMES

"I SEE SOMETHING YOU DON'T SEE, AND IT IS BLUE." Stuck for a way to get your youngsters to settle down in a museum? Sit them down on a bench in the middle of a room and play this vintage favorite. The leader gives just one clue—the color—and everybody guesses away.

"I'M GOING TO THE GROCERY..." The first player begins, "I'm going to the grocery and I'm going to buy... " and finishes the sentence with the name of an object, found in grocery stores, that begins with the letter "A." The second player repeats what the first player has said, and adds the name of another item that starts with "B." The third player repeats everything that has been said so far and adds something that begins with "C" and so on through the alphabet. Anyone who skips or misremembers an item is out (or decide up front that you'll give hints to all who need 'em). You can modify the theme depending on where you're going that day, as "I'm going to X and I'm going to see..."

FAMILY ARK Noah had his ark—here's your chance to build your own. It's easy. Just start naming animals and work your way through the alphabet, from antelope to zebra.

NOT THE GOOFY GAME Have one child name a category. (Some ideas: first names, last names, animals, countries, friends, feelings, foods, hot or cold things, clothing.) Then take turns naming things that fall into that category. You're out if you name something that doesn't belong in the category—or if you can't think of another item to name. When only one person remains, start again. Choose categories depending on where you're going or where you've been—historic topics if you've seen a historic sight, animal topics before or after the zoo, upside-down things if you've been to the circus, and so on. Make the game harder by choosing category items in A-B-C order.

DRUTHERS How do your kids really feel about things? Just ask. "Would you rather eat worms or hamburgers? Hamburgers or candy?" Choose serious and silly topics—and have fun!

BUILD A STORY "Once upon a time there lived..." Finish the sentence and ask the rest of your family, one at a time, to add another sentence or two. Bring a tape recorder along to record the narrative—and you can enjoy your creation again and again.

GOOD TIMES GALORE

WIGGLE & GIGGLE Give your kids a chance to stick out their tongues at you. Start by making a face, then have the next person imitate you and add a gesture of his own—snapping fingers, winking, clapping, sneezing, or the like. The next person mimics the first two and adds a third gesture, and so on.

JUNIOR OPERA During a designated period of time, have your kids sing everything they want to say.

THE QUIET GAME Need a good giggle—or a moment of calm to figure out your route? The driver sets a time limit and everybody must be silent. The last person to make a sound wins.

HIGH FIVES

BEST IN TOWN
Bronx Zoo
New York Botanical Garden
Central Park
New York Hall of Science
Ellis Island

BEST OUTDOORS
Rye Playland

BEST CULTURAL ACTIVITY
Broadway on a Budget

BEST MUSEUM
American Museum of Natural History

WACKIEST
Sony Wonder Technology Lab

NEW & NOTEWORTHY
Madame Tussaud's Wax Museum

SOMETHING FOR EVERYONE

ART ATTACK
American Folk Art Museum 68
Brooklyn Museum of Art 59
Children's Museum of the Arts 52
Forbes Magazine Galleries 44
Jewish Museum 40
Metropolitan Museum of Art 34
Museum of Modern Art 33
National Museum of the American Indian 30

COOL 'HOODS
Broadway on a Budget 64
Lower East Side Tenement Museum 37
South Street Seaport Museum 6

FARMS AND ANIMALS
Bronx Zoo 63
Central Park Zoo 55
Prospect Park Zoo 15
Queens County Farm Museum 13
Queens Zoo 12
Staten Island Zoo 4

FREEBIES
American Folk Art Museum 68
Clay Pit Ponds State Park Reserve 51
Forbes Magazine Galleries 44
National Museum of the American Indian 30
New York Unearthed 19
Queens County Farm Museum 13
Schomburg Center 8
Sony Wonder Technology Lab 7

GAMES AND AMUSEMENTS
Chelsea Piers 54
Coney Island 49
PlaySpace 17
Rye Playland 9

GOOD SPORTS
Asphalt Green 65
Chelsea Piers 54
F.A.O. Schwarz 46
Madison Square Garden 35

New York Liberty Basketball 21
PlaySpace 17
Rockefeller Center and the Ice Rink 10

HISTORICAL
American Museum of Natural History 67
Ellis Island 48
Federal Hall National Memorial 45
Fraunces Tavern Museum 43
Historic Richmond Town 42
Museum of the City of New York 31
New-York Historical Society 22
Schomburg Center 8
Theodore Roosevelt Birthplace 2
United Nations 1

PARKS AND GARDENS
Brooklyn Botanic Garden 61
Central Park 56
Clay Pit Ponds State Park Reserve 51
Jones Beach State Park 39
New York Botanical Garden 26
Prospect Park 16

PLANES, TRAINS, AND AUTOMOBILES (AND TRUCKS)
Intrepid Sea Air Space Museum 41
New York City Fire Museum 25
New York Transit Museum 20

SCIENTIFIC TERRIFIC
American Museum of Natural History 67
Liberty Science Center 38
New York Hall of Science 23
New York Unearthed 19
Sony Wonder Technology Lab 7
South Street Seaport Museum 6

SHOW TIME
American Museum of the Moving Image 66
Broadway on a Budget 64
Brooklyn Academy of Music 62
Carnegie Hall 58
Colden Center for the Performing Arts 50
Museum of Television and Radio 32

New Victory Theater **28**
New York City Opera Young People's Workshops **24**
Puppetworks **14**
Radio City Music Hall **11**

TERRIFIC TOURS
Intrepid Sea Air Space Museum **41**
Madison Square Garden **35**
NBC Studios Backstage Tour **29**
Radio City Music Hall **11**

TINIEST TOTS
Brooklyn Children's Museum **60**
Children's Museum of Manhattan **53**
Children's Museum of the Arts **52**
F.A.O. Schwarz **46**
PlaySpace **17**
Rye Playland **9**
Staten Island Children's Museum **5**

WATER, WATER EVERYWHERE
Asphalt Green **65**
Chelsea Piers **54**
Coney Island **49**
Jones Beach State Park **39**
New York Aquarium **27**
NY Waterway Ferries **18**
Rye Playland **9**
South Street Seaport Museum **6**

WAY UP HIGH
Castle Clinton National Monument **57**
Empire State Building **47**
Statue of Liberty **3**

WEIRD AND WACKY
Madame Tussaud's Wax Museum **36**
Sony Wonder Technology Lab **7**

ALL AROUND TOWN

BATTERY PARK
Castle Clinton National Monument **57**
National Museum of the American Indian **30**
New York Unearthed **19**

BROADWAY
Broadway on a Budget **64**
Madame Tussaud's Wax Museum **36**
New Victory Theater **28**

BRONX
Bronx Zoo **63**
New York Botanical Garden **26**

BROOKLYN
Brooklyn Academy of Music **62**
Brooklyn Botanic Garden **61**
Brooklyn Children's Museum **60**
Brooklyn Museum of Art **59**
Coney Island **49**
New York Aquarium **27**
New York Transit Museum **20**
Prospect Park **16**
Prospect Park Zoo **15**
Puppetworks **14**

CENTRAL PARK
American Folk Art Museum **68**
Central Park **56**
Central Park Zoo **55**

CHELSEA
Chelsea Piers **54**

FLATIRON DISTRICT
Theodore Roosevelt Birthplace **2**

GARMENT DISTRICT
Madison Square Garden **35**
New York Liberty Basketball **21**

GREENWICH VILLAGE
Forbes Magazine Galleries **44**
Puppetworks **14**

HARLEM
Schomburg Center **8**

LINCOLN CENTER
American Folk Art Museum **68**
New York City Opera Young People's
Workshops **24**

LONG ISLAND
Jones Beach State Park **39**

LOWER EAST SIDE
Lower East Side Tenement Museum **37**

MIDTOWN
Carnegie Hall **58**
F.A.O. Schwarz **46**
Intrepid Sea Air Space Museum **41**
Sony Wonder Technology Lab **7**
United Nations **1**

MURRAY HILL
Empire State Building **47**

NEW JERSEY
Liberty Science Center **38**

NEW YORK HARBOR
Ellis Island **48**
Statue of Liberty **3**

QUEENS
American Museum of the Moving Image **66**
Colden Center for the Performing Arts **50**

Museum of Modern Art **33**
New York Hall of Science **23**
Queens County Farm Museum **13**
Queens Zoo **12**

ROCKEFELLER CENTER
Museum of Modern Art **33**
Museum of Television and Radio **32**
NBC Studios Backstage Tour **29**
Radio City Music Hall **11**
Rockefeller Center and the Ice Rink **10**

THE SEAPORT
South Street Seaport Museum **6**

SOHO
Children's Museum of the Arts **52**
New York City Fire Museum **25**

STATEN ISLAND
Clay Pit Ponds State Park Preserve **51**
Historic Richmond Town **42**
Staten Island Children's Museum **5**
Staten Island Zoo **4**

UPPER EAST SIDE/
MUSEUM MILE
Asphalt Green **65**
Jewish Museum **40**
Metropolitan Museum of Art **34**
Museum of the City of New York **31**

UPPER WEST SIDE
American Museum of Natural History **67**
Children's Museum of Manhattan **53**

New-York Historical Society **22**
PlaySpace **17**

WALL STREET
Federal Hall National Memorial **45**
Fraunces Tavern Museum **43**

WESTCHESTER
Rye Playland **9**

MANY THANKS

In the '70s, my boyfriend—now husband—and I would joke that we were off on another "family adventure" as we explored parks, museums, and other attractions. No family, of course. Today, more than a quarter of a century later, we still take those family adventures, but now with three children in tow. As a parent, a teacher, and writer, I look for those "teachable moments" to share with my children. I must confess that with a 5-year-old, a 12-year-old, and a 14-year-old, it is often challenging to find something of interest for everyone, parents included. This book was written with that in mind.

Many thanks to the public relations professionals at each of our sights who were so helpful in answering questions and checking facts. This book is lovingly dedicated to Rachel ("Are we there yet?"); Jennifer ("Can we listen to the car radio instead of those children's tapes?"); and Michael ("When are we leaving?").

— Mindy Bailin